Cracking MATHS
Senior Infants

**Majella O'Connor, Aishling Doyle,
Joan Gilligan, Carmel Kelly, Catherine Knight**

g GILL EDUCATION

GW00402425

Gill Education
Hume Avenue
Park West
Dublin 12
www.gilleducation.ie

Gill Education is an imprint of M.H. Gill & Co

ISBN: 978 07171 54234

Design: Outburst Design and Richard Jervis

Internal illustrations: Kate Shannon

Technical drawings: MPS Limited

Cover illustration: www.designbos.ie

Consultant editor in mathematics curriculum and pedagogy: Betty Stoutt

Mathematics consultant: Oliver Hyde

For permission to reproduce photographs, the authors and publisher gratefully
acknowledge the following:

© Alamy: 20TL; © iStock: 31L, 50L, 66L, 77L, 78, 94; © Shutterstock: 19, 20TR, 20BL, 20BR,
21, 31R, 50R, 66R, 77R, 100, 112, 131, 133, 134, 136, 137, 140.

The paper used in this book comes from the wood pulp of sustainably managed forests.

Any links to external websites should not be construed as an endorsement by Gill
Education of the content or view of the linked material.

The publishers have made every effort to contact copyright holders but any omissions
will be rectified at the next reprint.

Contents

1. Look Back – Early Mathematical Activities

Match

Strand: Early Mathematical Activities
Curriculum objectives:
Match equivalent and non-equivalent sets using one-to-one correspondence;
order objects according to length or height;
order sets without counting.

Match

1. Ring the one that is the same.

Sort

1. **Colour the fish** yellow. **Colour the animals** red.
Colour the plants green.

Sort

1. **Colour the one that is different.**

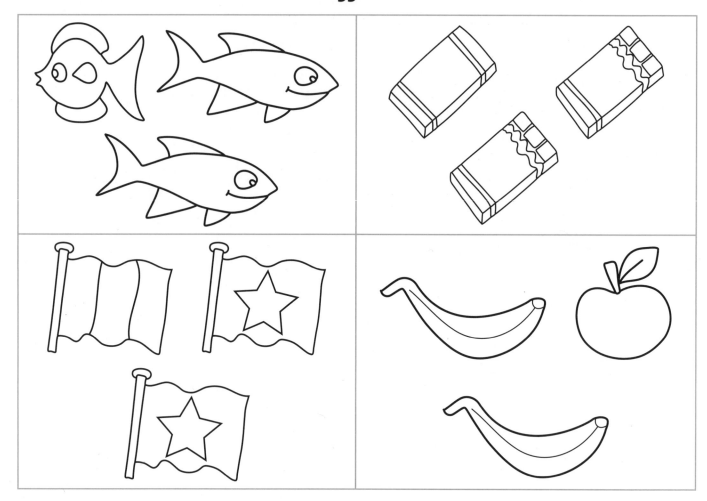

2. **Ring the things that do not belong in the picnic basket.**

Order

1. **Colour the sets that have the most blue.**
   Colour the sets that have the least green.

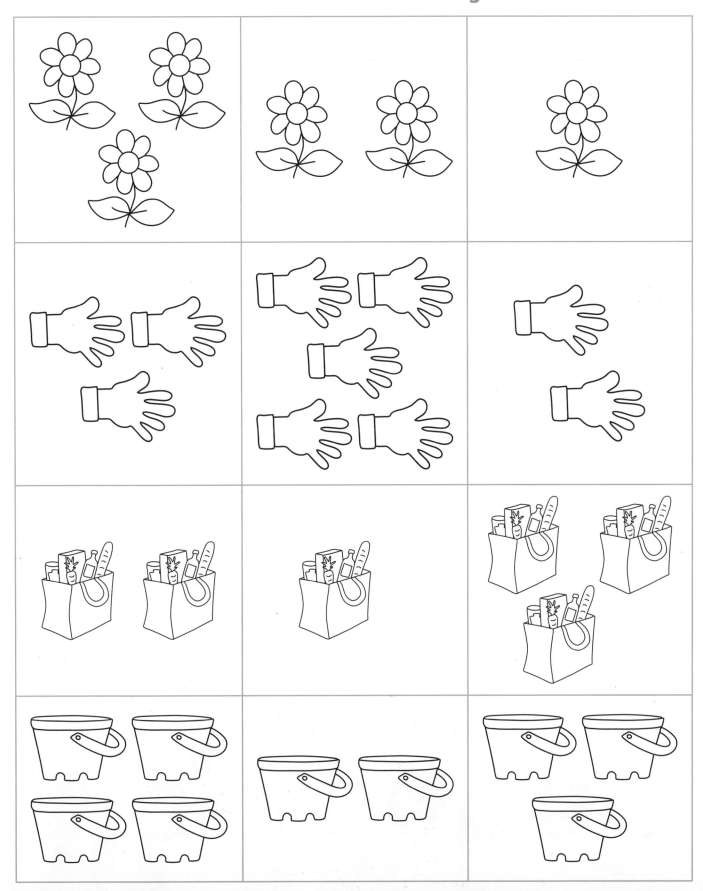

Draw

1. **Make each set the same.**

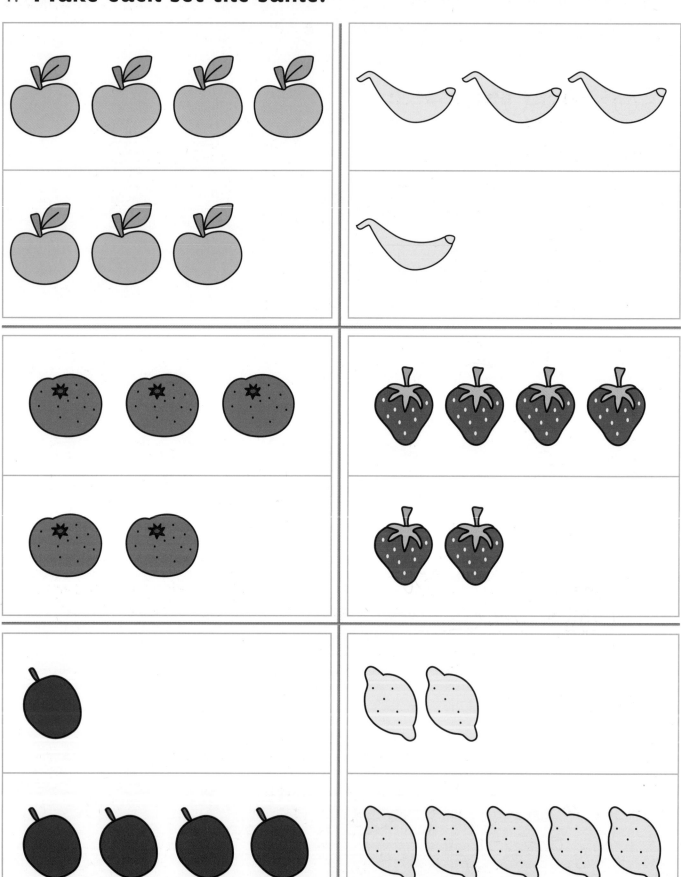

2. Look Back

Count

1. **Ring, count and match.**

2. 0 0 0 0 0 0 0 0 0 0 0 0

Curriculum objectives:
To revise concepts that were explored in Junior Infants.

Count

1. Draw the correct number of  **balloons.**

2.

Count

I. How many? Write the numeral.

2. 2 2 2 2 2 2 2 2 2 2 2

Count

I. **Count. Write the correct numeral in the box.**

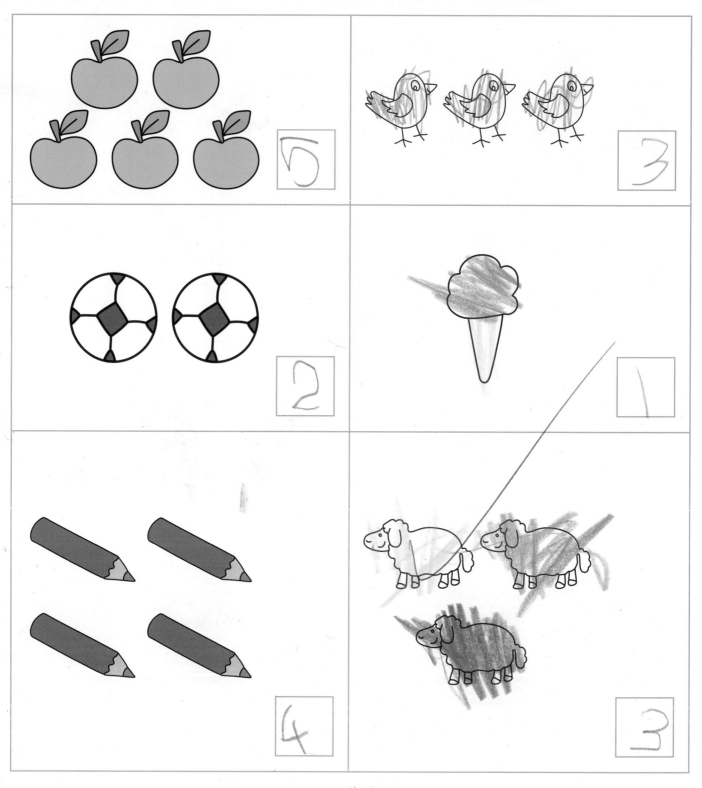

2.

Count

1. **Count. Write the correct numeral.**

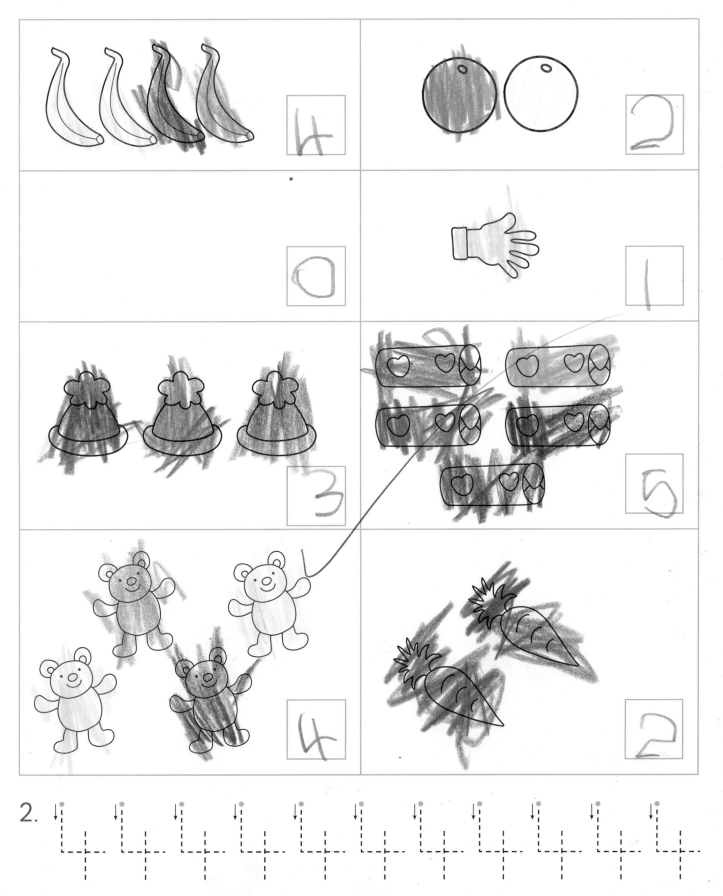

2.

Draw Spots on the Ladybirds

1.

4 spots

3 spots

5 spots

4 spots

2 spots

2. 5 5 5 5 5 5 5 5 5 5

Add

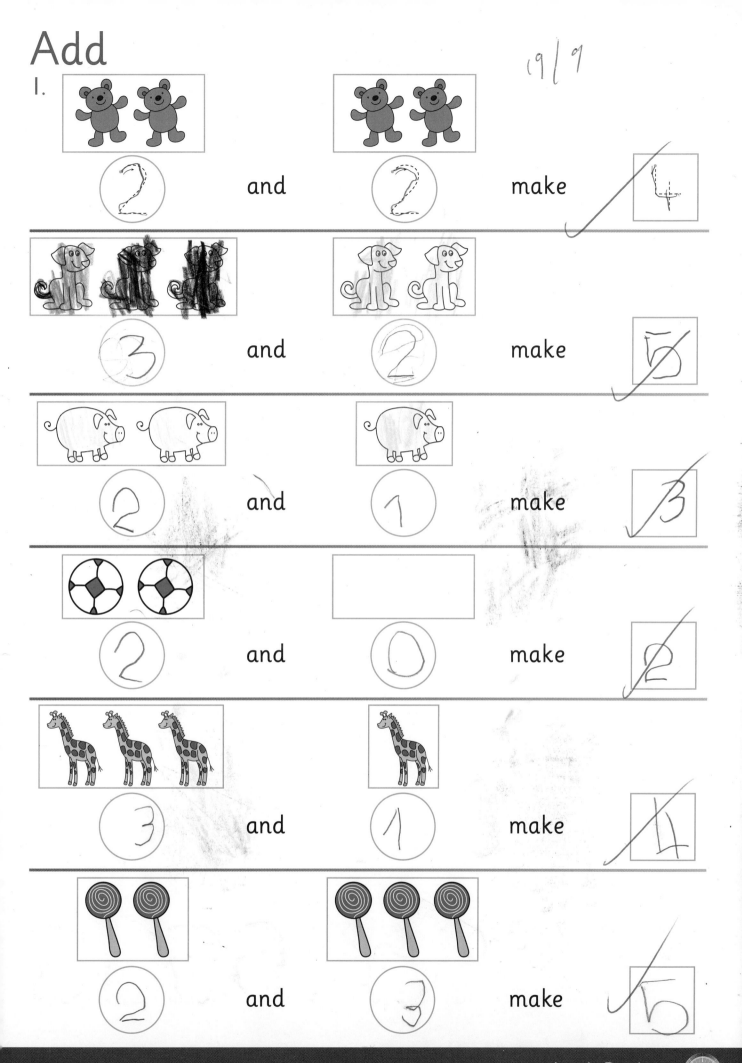

1.

2 and 2 make 4

3 and 2 make 5

2 and 1 make 3

2 and 0 make 2

3 and 1 make 4

2 and 3 make 5

19/9

Add

I.

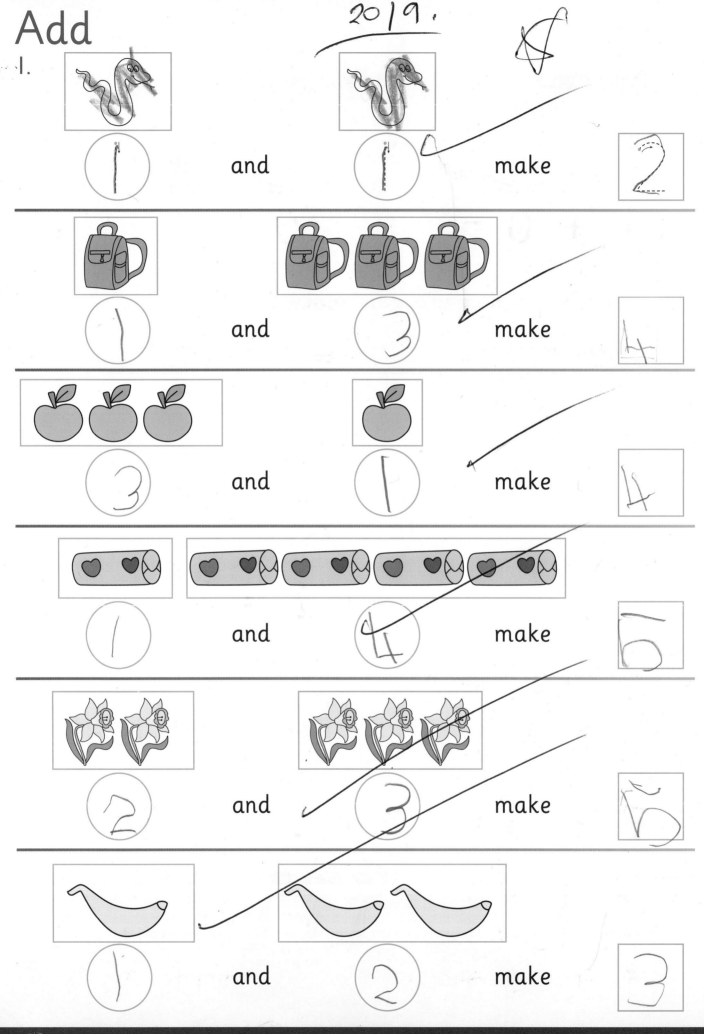

and make 2

and 3 make 4

3 and 1 make 4

1 and 4 make 5

2 and 3 make 5

1 and 2 make 3

Write

1. **How many ways can you make 1?**

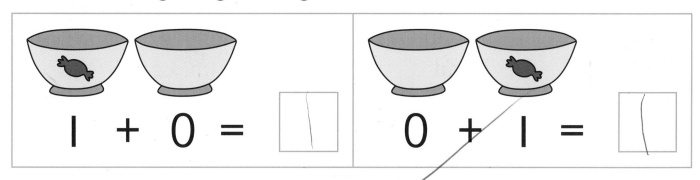

$1 + 0 = \boxed{1}$ $0 + 1 = \boxed{1}$

2. **How many ways can you make 2?**

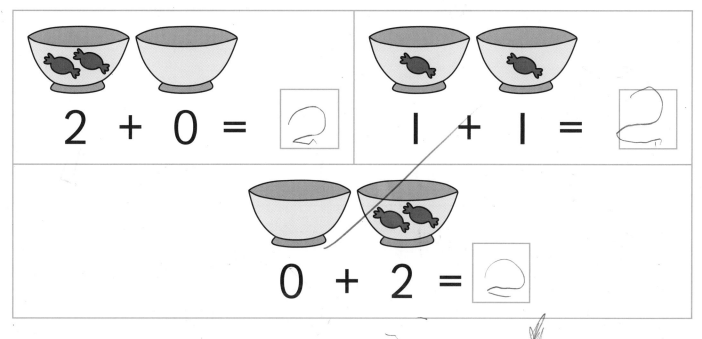

$2 + 0 = \boxed{2}$ $1 + 1 = \boxed{2}$

$0 + 2 = \boxed{2}$

3. **How many ways can you make 3?**

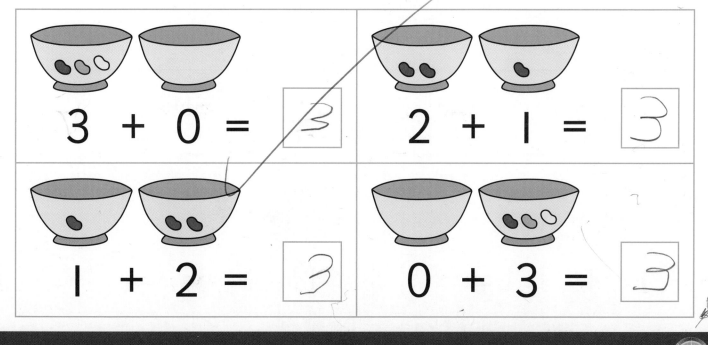

$3 + 0 = \boxed{3}$ $2 + 1 = \boxed{3}$

$1 + 2 = \boxed{3}$ $0 + 3 = \boxed{3}$

Write

23/9

1. How many ways can you make 4?

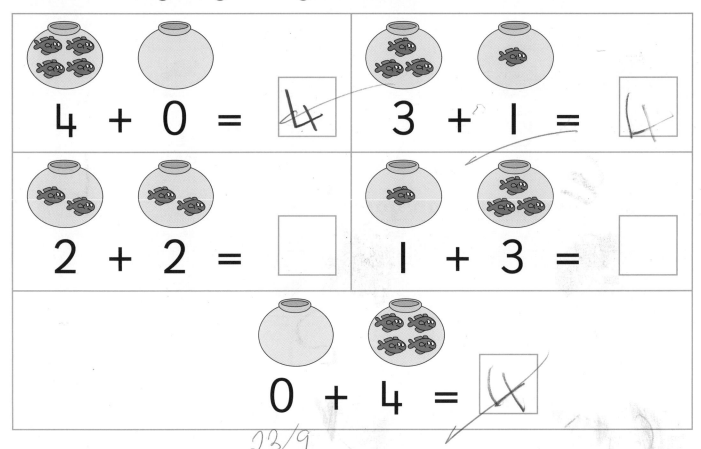

4 + 0 = 4

3 + 1 = 5

2 + 2 =

1 + 3 =

0 + 4 = 4

23/9

2. How many ways can you make 5?

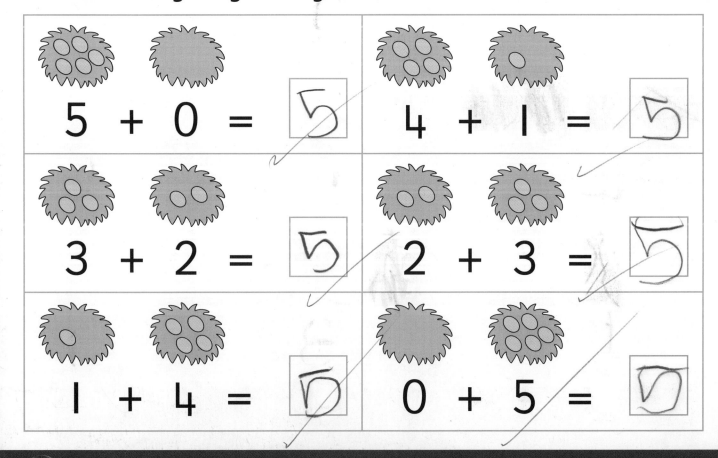

5 + 0 = 5

4 + 1 = 5

3 + 2 = 5

2 + 3 = 5

1 + 4 = 5

0 + 5 = 5

Add

3

1.

and ① make 4

and ① make 3

and ② make ~~6~~

and ④ make ~~5~~

and ① make ~~4~~

Strand: Number
Curriculum objectives:
Count the number of objects in a set, 0–10;
explore the components of number, 1–10;
combine sets of objects, totals to 10;
read, write and order numerals, 0–10;

identify the empty set and the numeral zero;
estimate the number of objects in a set, 2–10;
solve simple oral and pictorial problems, 0–10;
develop an understanding of the conservation of number, 0–10;
partition sets of objects, 0–10;
use the symbols + and = to construct word sentences involving addition.

17

Starfish on a Beach

I. **Write the correct numeral. Add.**

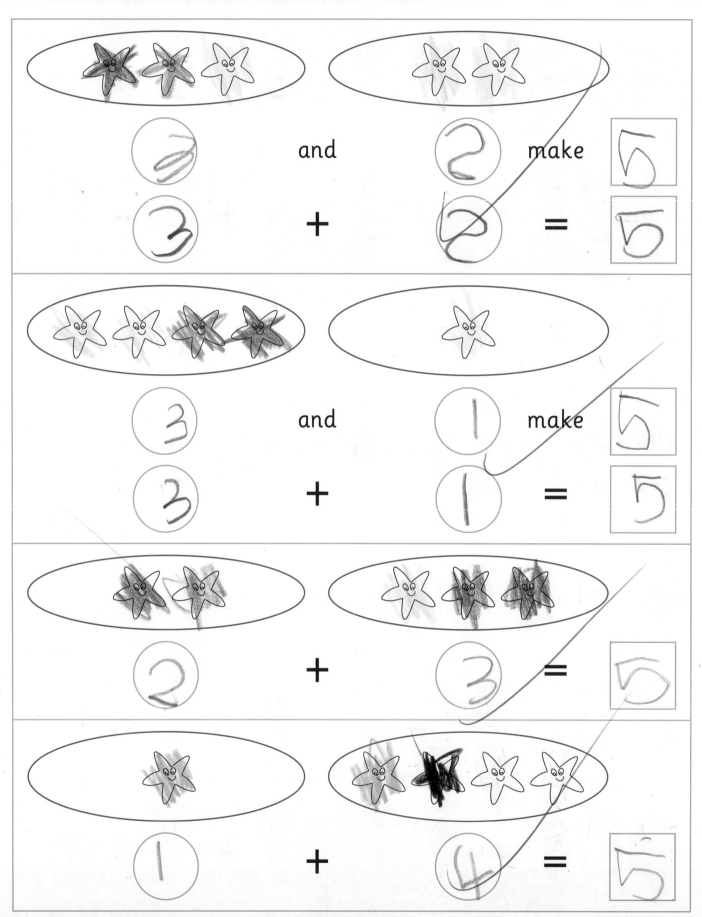

and $3 + 2 =$ make 5 5

and $3 + 1 =$ make 5 5

$2 + 3 = 5$

$1 + 4 = 5$

Add

Use your cubes.

1. **How many Easter eggs?**

 and  $3 + 2 = 5$

  and $4 + 1 = 5$

 and  $1 + 3 = 4$

 and  $2 + 3 = 5$

 and  $1 + 4 = 5$

 and  $2 + 2 = 4$

 and $3 + 1 = 4$

Zero 0

1. Why is Zero hungry?

2. Write the numeral 0.

How Many Crabs?

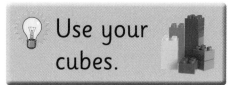
1. **Write the correct numeral. Add.**

3/10

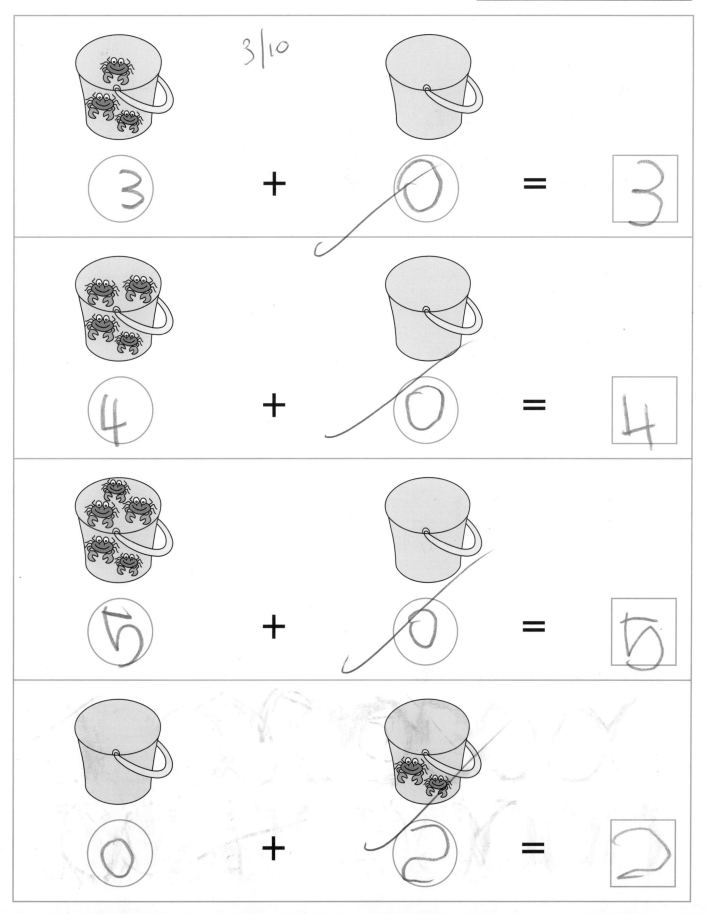

3 + 0 = 3

4 + 0 = 4

5 + 0 = 5

0 + 2 = 2

Make 5

1. **We need 5 counters in each group. Draw the missing counters in the bowl.**

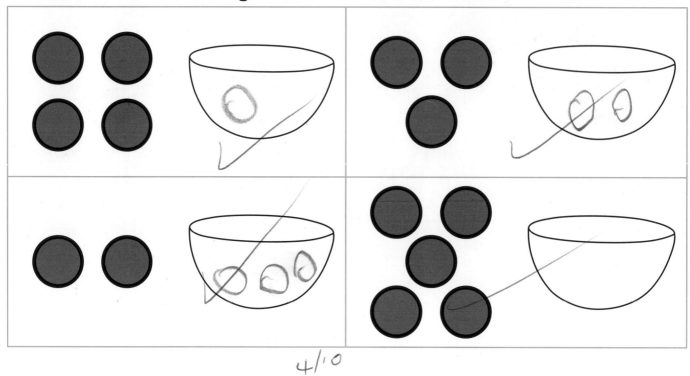

4/10

2. **How many ways can you make 5?**

▦▦▦▦▦	$5 + 0 = 5$
▦▦▦▦☐	$4 + 1 = 5$
▦▦▦☐☐	$3 + 2 = 5$
▦▦☐☐☐	$2 + 3 = 5$
▦☐☐☐☐	$1 + 4 = 5$
☐☐☐☐☐	$0 + 5 = 5$

3. **Colour the books that make 5.**

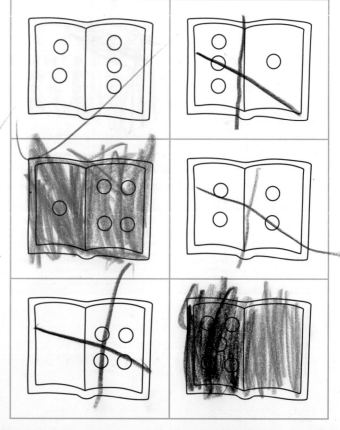

What Makes 5? +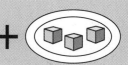

How many ways can you make 5?

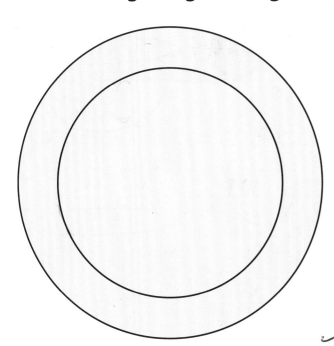

5/10

+

1.
$5 + 0 = 5$

$4 + 1 = 5$

$3 + 2 = 5$

$2 + 3 = 5$

$1 + 4 = 5$

$0 + 5 = 5$

2. Colour 5 with two of your favourite colours.

4. Number 6

6 six

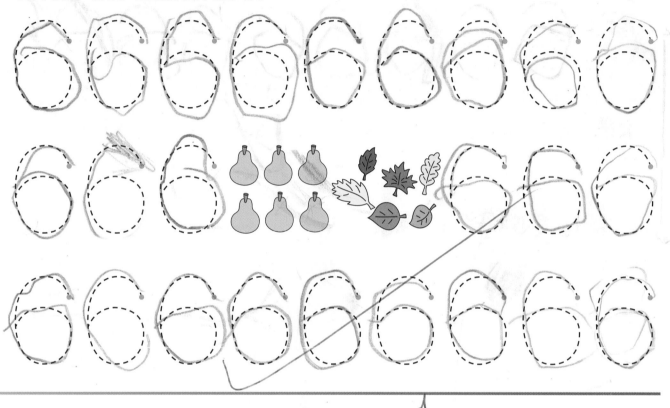

1. **Write the numeral 6.**

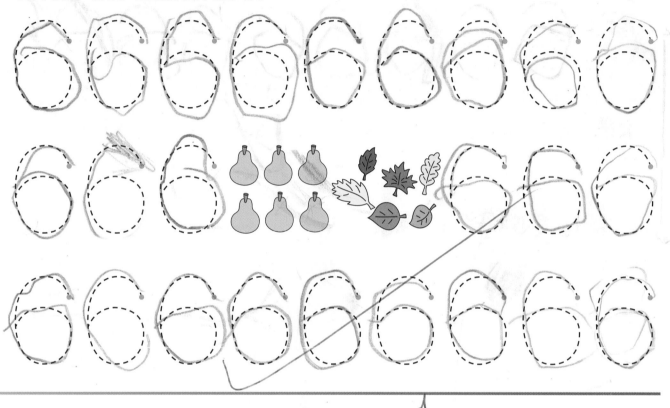

2. **Colour 6 acorns.**

V.good
6/10

Strand: Number
Curriculum objectives:
Count the number of objects in a set, 0–10;
explore the components of number, 1–10;
combine sets of objects, totals to 10;
read, write and order numerals, 0–10;
identify the empty set and the numeral zero;
estimate the number of objects in a set, 2–10;
solve simple oral and pictorial problems, 0–10;
develop an understanding of the conservation of number, 0–10;
partition sets of objects, 0–10;
use the symbols + and = to construct word sentences involving addition.

6 six

 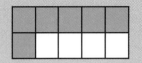

1. Write the numeral 6.

6 6 6 6 6 6 6 6 6 6

6 6 6 6 6 6 6 6 6 6

2. Ring the sets of 6.

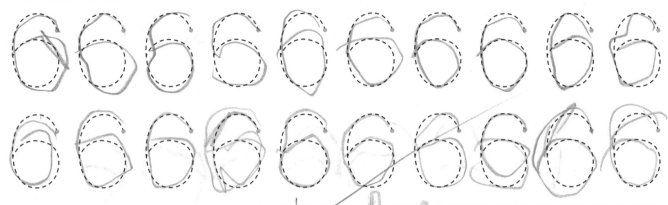

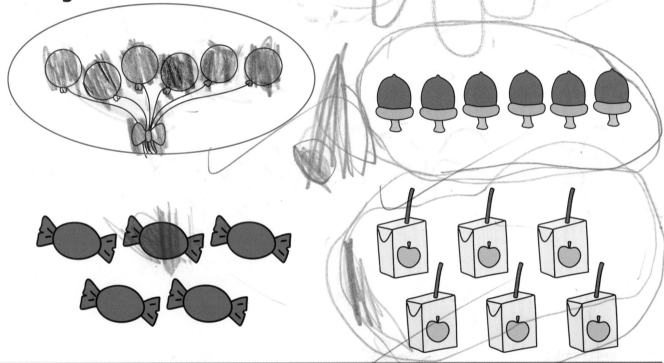

3. Draw 6 balloons.

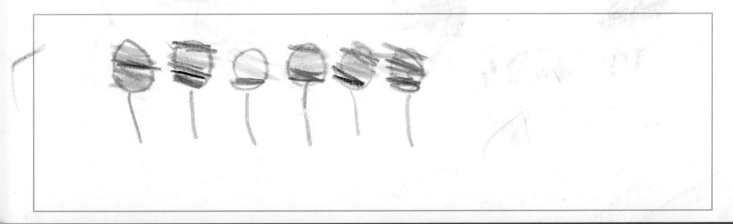

Count and Match

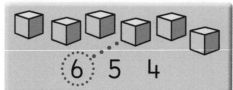

1.

4 5 6	4 5 6
4 5 6	4 5 6
4 5 6	4 5 6

Make 6

1. **Draw more balls to make 6.**
   Colour.

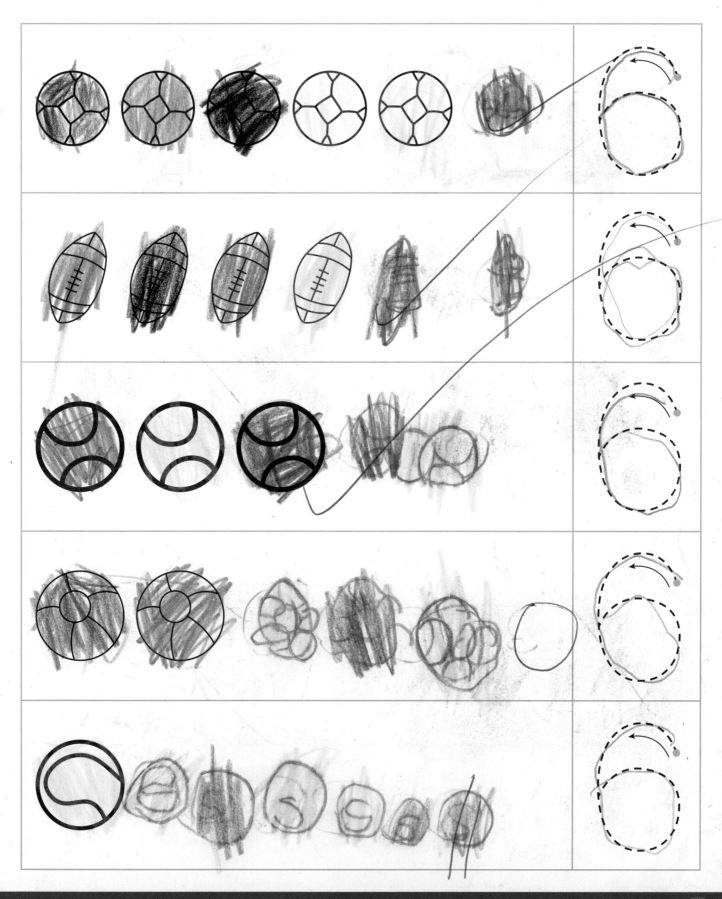

Make 6

1. Colour the acorns green. Write the number sentence.

$6 + 0 = 6$

$5 + 1 = 6$

$4 + 2 = 6$

$3 + 3 = 6$

$2 + 4 = 6$

$1 + 5 = 6$

$0 + 6 = 6$

What Makes 6?

How many ways can you make 6?

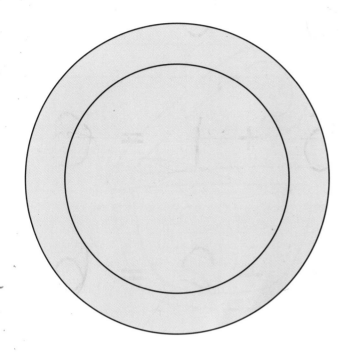 +

1.

 = 6

 = 6

3 + 3 = 6

4 + 2 = 6

5 + 1 = 6

 = 6

4 + 4 = 6

2. **Colour 6 with two of your favourite colours.**

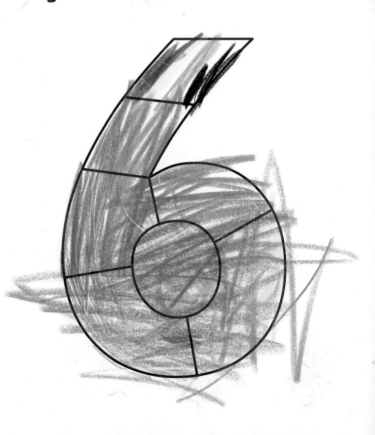

Make 6

Put 6 counters on the sunglasses in different ways.

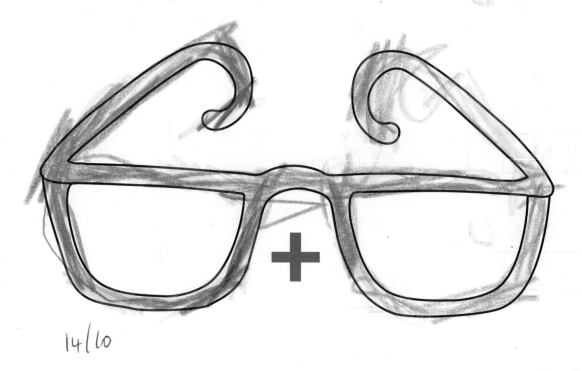

14/10

1.

0	+	6	= 6
1	+	5	= 6
2	+	4	= 6
3	+	3	= 6
4	+	2	= 6
5	+	1	= 6
6	+	0	= 6

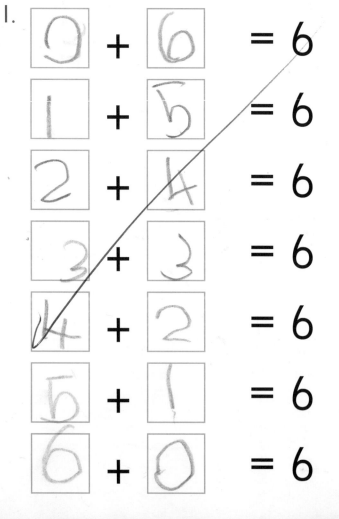

2. **Colour the glasses that make 6.**

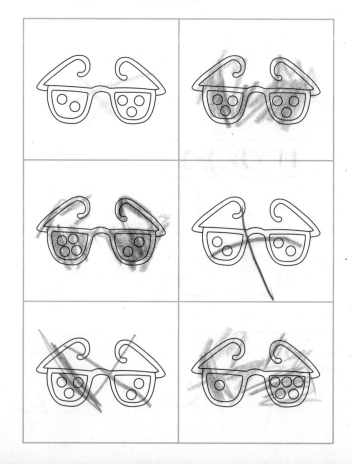

Add

1. Draw the counters.

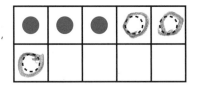

$$3 + 3 = 6$$

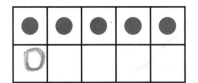

$$5 + 1 = 6$$

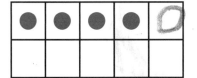

$$4 + 0 = 5$$

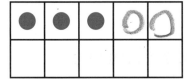

$$3 + 2 = 5$$

$$2 + 4 = 4$$

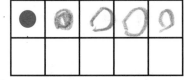

$$1 + 5 = 6$$

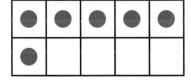

$$6 + 0 = 6$$

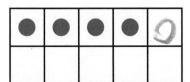

$$4 + 1 = 5$$

Add

1. Colour the books.

💡 Use your ten frame and cubes to help you.

4 blue   5 red   6 green

2. Count and ring the correct numeral.

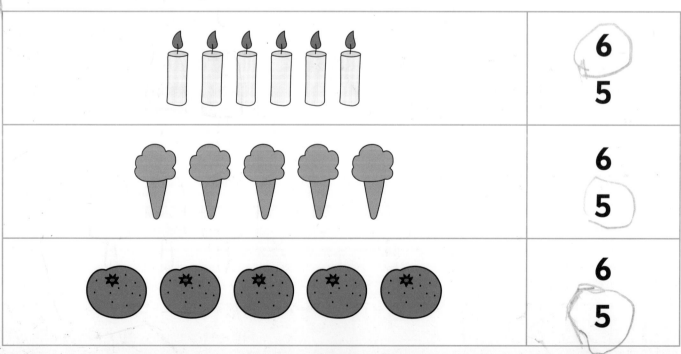

5. Extending Patterns

Colour

1. **Finish the pattern. Colour the last ice-pop.**

24/10 Great!

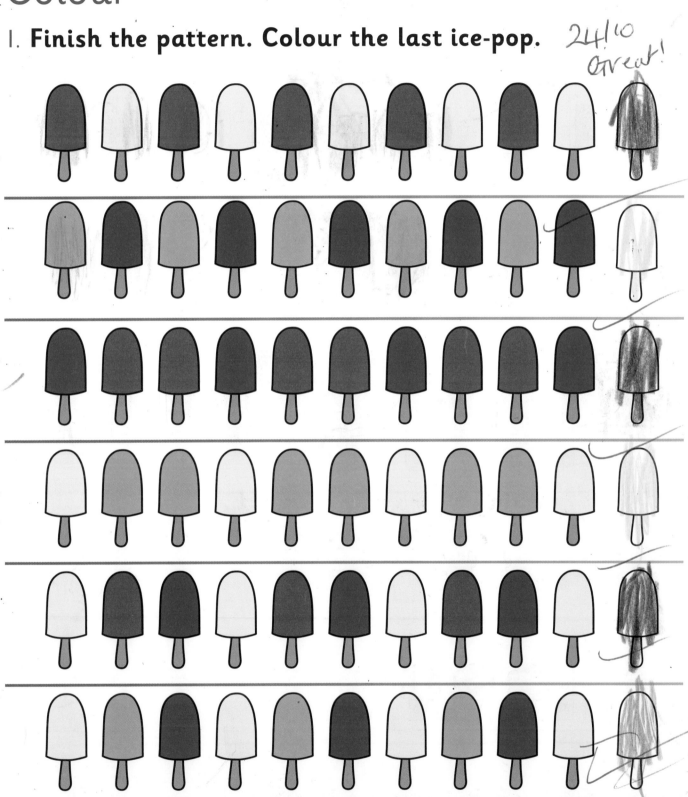

Strand: Algebra
Curriculum objectives:
Identify, copy and extend pattern in colour, shape, size and number;
discover different arrays of the same number;
recognise patterns and predict subsequent number.

33

Pattern

25/10.

1. Colour. Finish the pattern.

2. Draw. Finish the pattern.

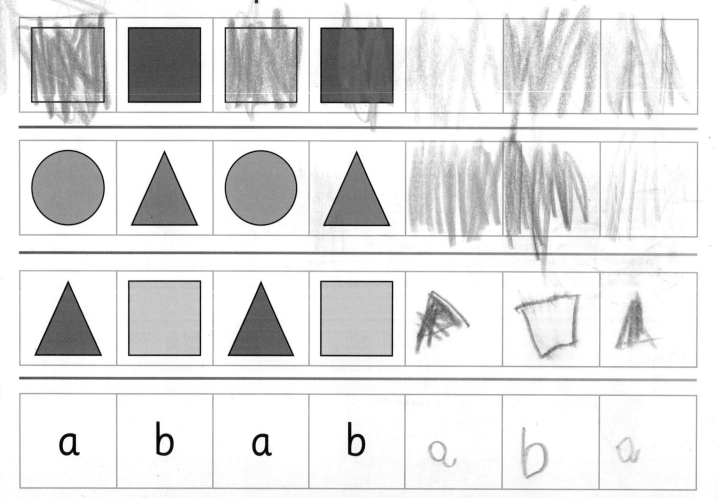

| a | b | a | b | a | b | a |

Pattern

1. Finish the pattern.

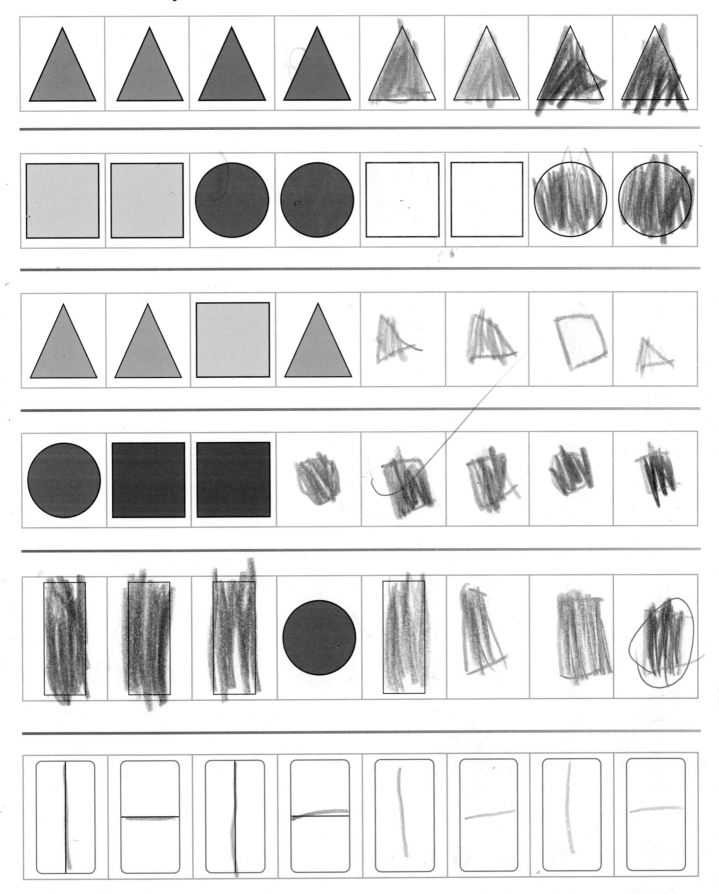

Pattern

1. Finish the pattern.

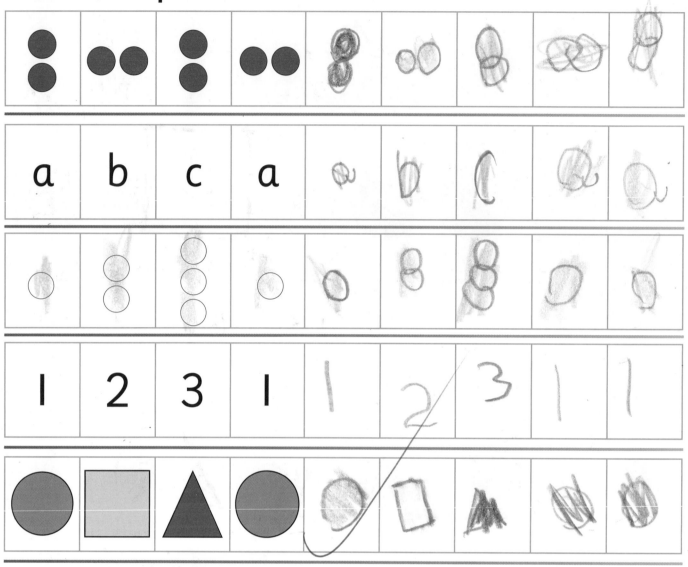

2. Ring what comes next.

6. 2-D Shapes

Mr Square and Miss Triangle

1. Here is Mr Square.

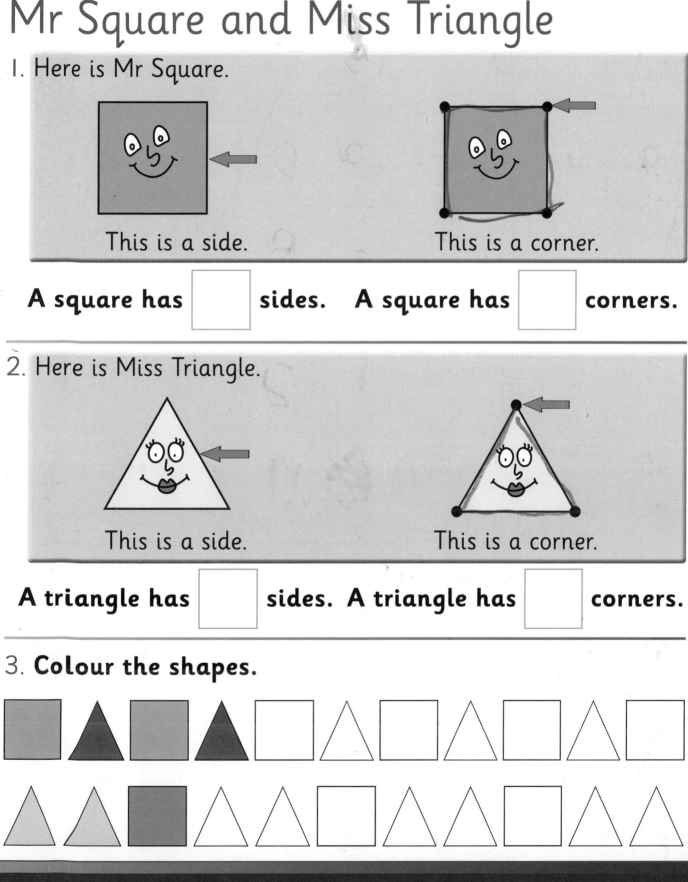

This is a side.

This is a corner.

A square has ☐ **sides.   A square has** ☐ **corners.**

2. Here is Miss Triangle.

This is a side.

This is a corner.

A triangle has ☐ **sides. A triangle has** ☐ **corners.**

3. **Colour the shapes.**

Strand: Shape and Space
Curriculum objectives:
Sort, describe and name 2-D shapes: square, circle, triangle, rectangle;
combine and divide 2-D shapes to make larger or smaller shapes;
solve problems involving shape and space.

Draw and Colour

1. **Join the corners and the sides on Miss Triangle. Colour the triangles.**

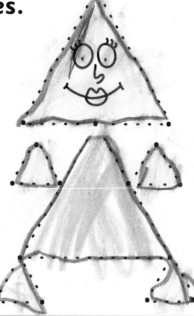

2. **Join the corners and the sides on Mr Square. Colour the squares.**

Art Attack

Cut paper shapes into two or four pieces and see what new shapes you make.

Mrs Circle and Mr Rectangle

Wow!

1. This is a circle. It has a curved side.

A circle has 1 **side.** **A circle has** 0 **corners.**

2. This is a rectangle. It has straight sides.

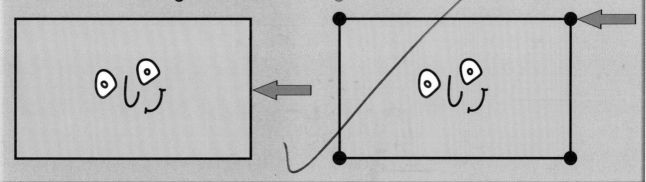

A rectangle has 4 **sides.** **A rectangle has** 4 **corners.**

3. | Draw a circle. | Draw a rectangle. |
|---|---|
|  |  |

Draw and Colour

1. **Join the curved sides on Mrs Circle.
   Colour the circles.**

2. **Join the corners and the sides on Mr Rectangle.
   Colour the rectangles.**

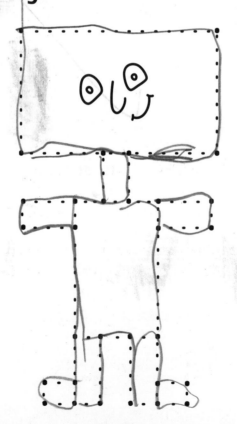

Draw and Colour

14|11

1. **Colour the kites above the clouds** yellow.
   Colour the kites below the clouds red.

2. **Draw a house to the right of the girl.**
   Draw a tree to the left of the girl.

3. **Colour the cows behind the fence** brown.

Strand: Shape and Space
Curriculum objectives:
Explore, discuss, develop and use the vocabulary of spatial relations.

8. Number 7

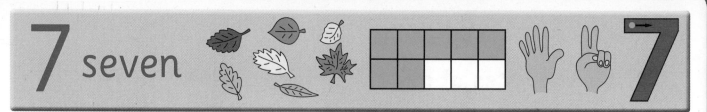

7 seven

1. Write the numeral 7.

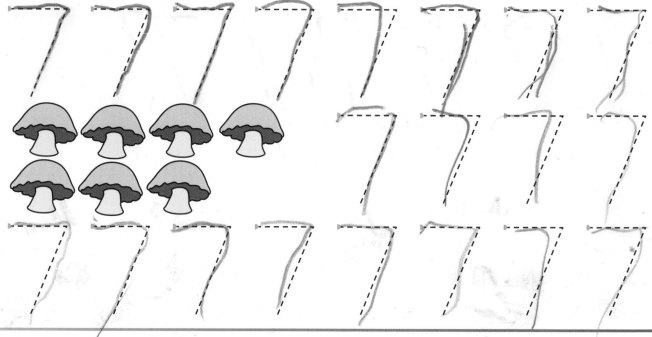

2. Colour 7 oak leaves.

15/11

Strand: Number
Curriculum objectives:
Count the number of objects in a set, 0–10;
explore the components of number, 1–10;
combine sets of objects, totals to 10;
read, write and order numerals, 0–10;

identify the empty set and the numeral zero;
estimate the number of objects in a set, 2–10;
solve simple oral and pictorial problems, 0–10;
develop an understanding of the conservation of number, 0–10;
partition sets of objects, 0–10;
use the symbols + and = to construct word sentences involving addition.

7 seven

 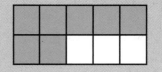

1. Write the numeral 7.

7 7 7 7 7 7 7 7

7 7 7 7 7 7 7 7

2. Ring and colour the sets of 7.

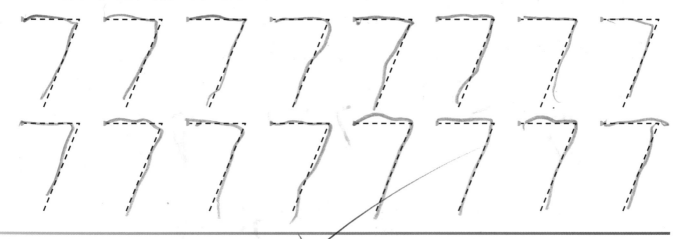

3. Draw 7 marbles.

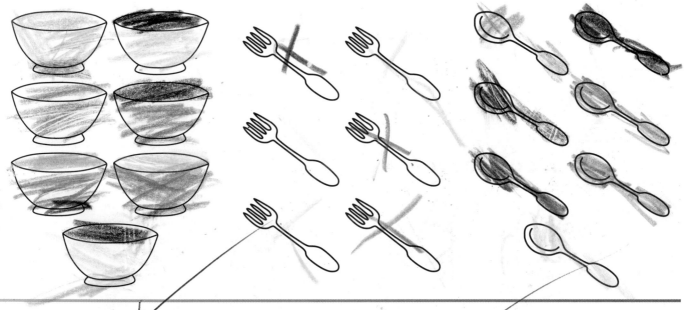

V_good
16/11

Count and Match

1.

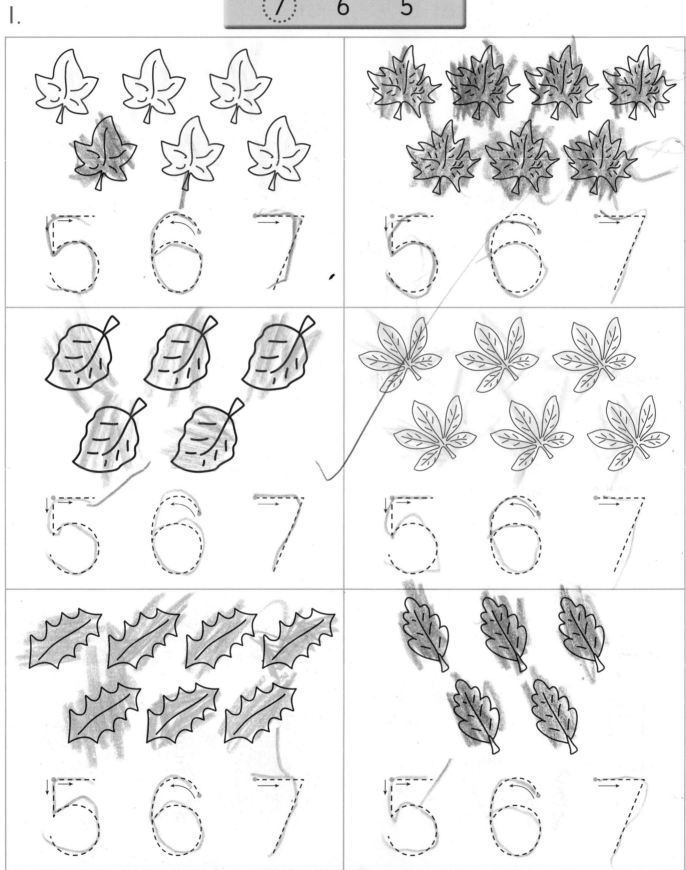

7

1. Ring and colour the groups of 7.

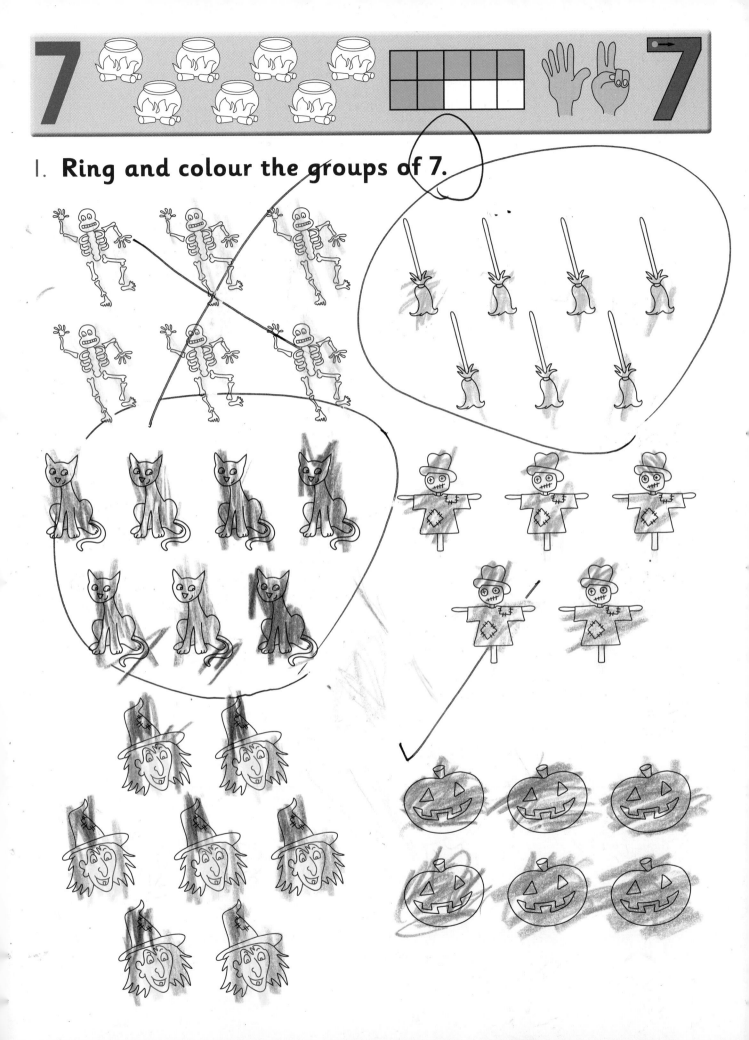

I. **Match to make 7.**

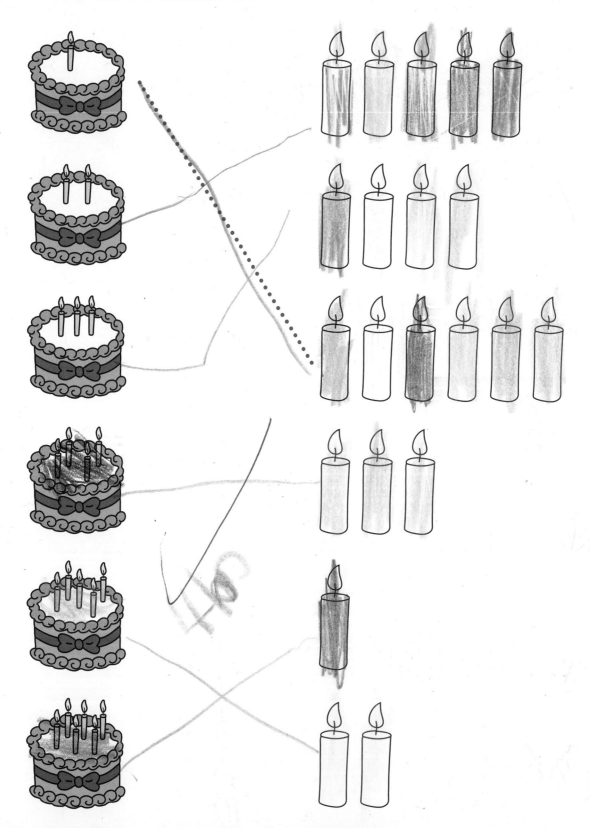

Make 7

1. Colour the leaves green. Write the number sentence.

$$7 + 0 = 7$$

$$6 + 1 = 7$$

$$5 + 2 = 7$$

$$4 + 3 = 7$$

$$3 + 4 = 7$$

$$2 + 4 = 7$$

$$1 + 6 = 7$$

$$0 + 7 = 7$$

What Makes 7?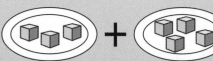

How many ways can you make 7?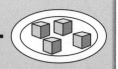

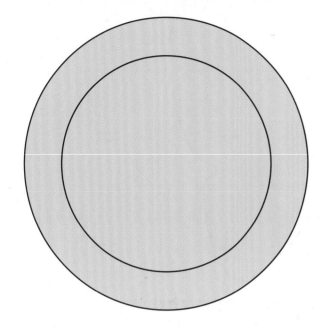 +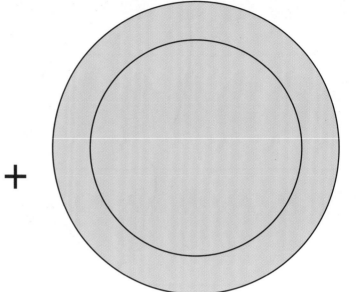

1.
☐ + ☐ = 7

☐ + ☐ = 7

☐ + ☐ = 7

☐ + ☐ = 7

☐ + ☐ = 7

☐ + ☐ = 7

☐ + ☐ = 7

☐ + ☐ = 7

2. Colour 7 with two of your favourite colours.

Make 7

Put 7 counters on the moth in different ways.

 Use counters to help you.

1.

$\boxed{} + \boxed{} = 7$

$\boxed{} + \boxed{} = 7$

$\boxed{} + \boxed{} = 7$

$\boxed{} + \boxed{} = 7$

$\boxed{} + \boxed{} = 7$

$\boxed{} + \boxed{} = 7$

$\boxed{} + \boxed{} = 7$

$\boxed{} + \boxed{} = 7$

2. **Colour the moths that make 7.**

Add

1. Draw the counters.

💡 Use cubes or counters to help you.

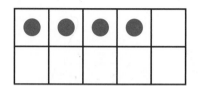

1	+	6	=	

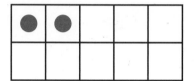

4	+	3	=	

2	+	4	=	

7	+	0	=	

5	+	2	=	

3	+	3	=	

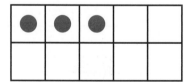

6	+	1	=	

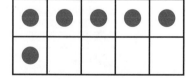

2	+	5	=	

Order

1. The Ugly Duckling

 1   2   3   4

2. Lego Fun

 5 4   2   1   3

3. Growing Up

 3 4   1   5 4   2

Strand: Measures
Curriculum objectives:
Develop an understanding of the concept of time through the use of appropriate vocabulary;
sequence daily and weekly events or stages in a story;
read time in one-hour intervals;
discuss significant times in the day;
understand the concept of time;
sequence the days of the week;
seasons, festivals and events relevant to seasons;
read and write time in hourly intervals.

51

Dan's Day

1. Look at what Dan did today.

8 o'clock	9 o'clock	1 o'clock	2 o'clock

5 o'clock	6 o'clock	7 o'clock	9 o'clock

2. Number the pictures in the correct order.

  3	 1	 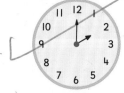 4	  2

Days of the Week

Monday   Tuesday   Wednesday   Thursday

Friday   Saturday   Sunday

1. **Write the correct day.**

Today is `ToDaY is` . Tuesday

Yesterday was `TuesDaYISTu` . Monday

Tomorrow will be `MOnDaY` .

I go to school on `MInday Do tosch` ,

`Tuesday` , `Wednes` ,

`Thursday` and `Friday` .

I do not go to school on `saturday` or

`sunday` .

My favourite day is _____ .

Days of the Week

1. Draw what you do at school each day.

Monday	Tuesday	Wednesday	Thursday	Friday

Today is <u>Wednasday</u>.

Yesterday was <u>Tuesday</u>.

Tomorrow will be <u>Thursday</u>.

2. Write the days.

I go to school on <u>Monday</u>.

I go to school on <u>Tuesday</u>.

I go to school on <u>Wednesda</u>.

I go to school on <u>Thursday</u>.

I go to school on <u>Friday</u>.

I do not go to school on <u>sundeay</u>.

I do not go to school on <u>satonday</u>.

Sunday
Monday
Tuesday
Wednesday
Thursday
Friday
Saturday

Seasons

1.

spring

summer

autumn

winter

2. **My birthday is in the season of** _____ .

What Time Is It?

2 o'clock

9 o'clock

4 o'clock

10 o'clock

7 o'clock

6 o'clock

1 o'clock

8 o'clock

3 o'clock

Draw the Hour Hand

2 o'clock

5 o'clock

8 o'clock

10 o'clock

6 o'clock

1 o'clock

4 o'clock

9 o'clock

7 o'clock

Time

1. Draw the hands on the clocks.

4 o'clock

3 o'clock

5 o'clock

9 o'clock

7 o'clock

6 o'clock

2. Draw the hands on the clocks.

early

on time

late

8 o'clock

9 o'clock

10 o'clock

10. Number 8

8 eight

1. Write the numeral 8.

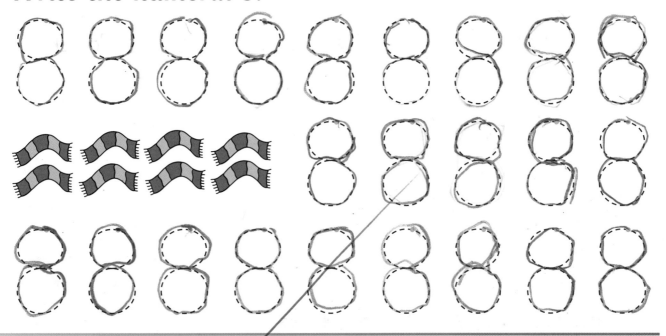

2. Colour 8 hats.

Excellent Work!

Strand: Number
Curriculum objectives:
Count the number of objects in a set, 0–10;
explore the components of number, 1–10;
combine sets of objects, totals to 10;
read, write and order numerals, 0–10;
identify the empty set and the numeral zero;
estimate the number of objects in a set, 2–10;
solve simple oral and pictorial problems, 0–10;
develop an understanding of the conservation of number, 0–10;
partition sets of objects, 0–10;
use the symbols + and = to construct word sentences involving addition.

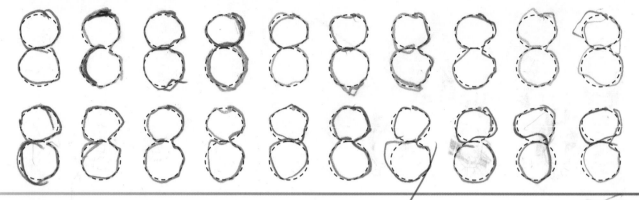

1. Write the numeral 8.

8 8 8 8 8 8 8 8 8 8

8 8 8 8 8 8 8 8 8 8

2. Ring the sets of 8.

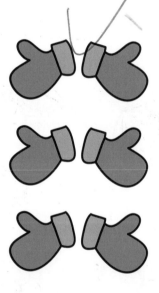

3. Draw 8 hats.

Count and Match

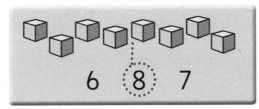

6 (8) 7

I.

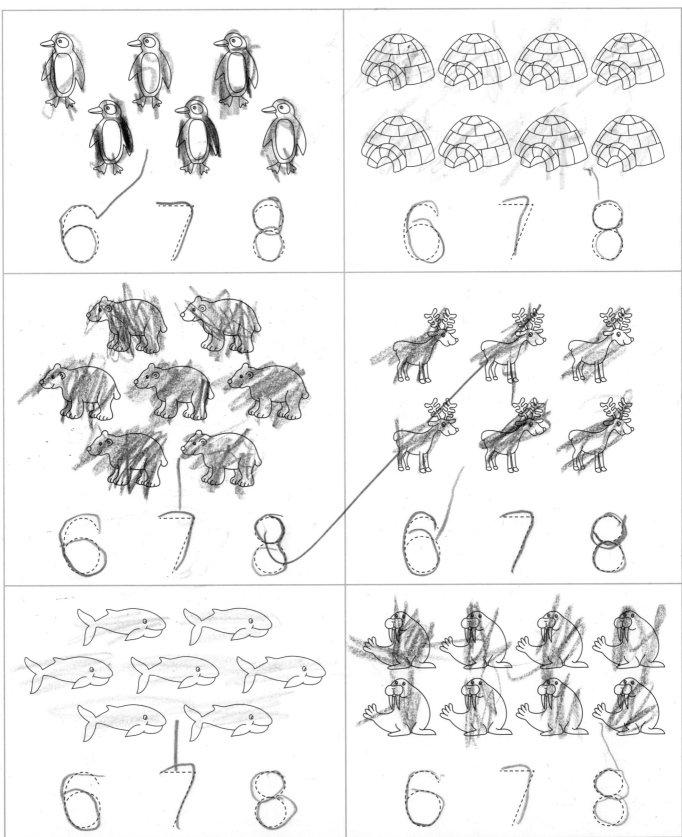

Draw

1. **Draw the correct number of balls for each clown.**

Make 8

1. Draw more clouds in each row to make 8.

What Makes 8?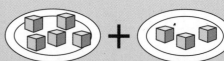

How many ways can you make 8?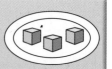

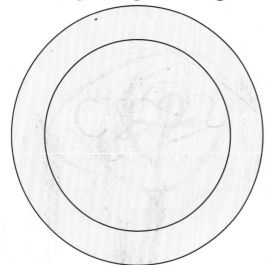 +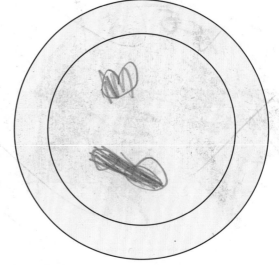

1.

$0 + 8 = 8$

$1 + 7 = 8$

$2 + 6 = 8$

$3 + 5 = 8$

$4 + 4 = 8$

$5 + 3 = 8$

$6 + 2 = 8$

$7 + 1 = 8$

$8 + 0 = 8$

2. **Colour 8 with two of your favourite colours.**

Make 8

Put 8 counters on the bat in different ways.

Use counters to help you.

1.

$\boxed{} + \boxed{8} = 8$

$\boxed{1} + \boxed{7} = 8$

$\boxed{2} + \boxed{6} = 8$

$\boxed{3} + \boxed{5} = 8$

$\boxed{4} + \boxed{4} = 8$

$\boxed{5} + \boxed{3} = 8$

$\boxed{6} + \boxed{2} = 8$

$\boxed{7} + \boxed{1} = 8$

$\boxed{8} + \boxed{0} = 8$

2. **Colour the bats that make 8.**

Add

1. Draw the counters.

 Use cubes or counters to help you.

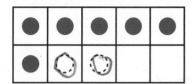

| 6 | + | 2 | = | 8 |

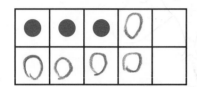

| 3 | + | 4 | = | 8 |

| 5 | + | 3 | = | 8 |

| 5 | + | 2 | = | 7 |

| 7 | + | 1 | = | 8 |

| 8 | + | 0 | = | 8 |

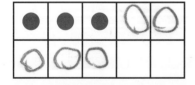

| 3 | + | 5 | = | 8 |

Excellent
13/12

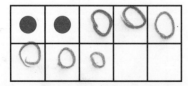

| 2 | + | 6 | = | 8 |

Add

1. **Match each elephant to the correct bucket of water.**

Use your ten frame and cubes to help you.

14 / 12

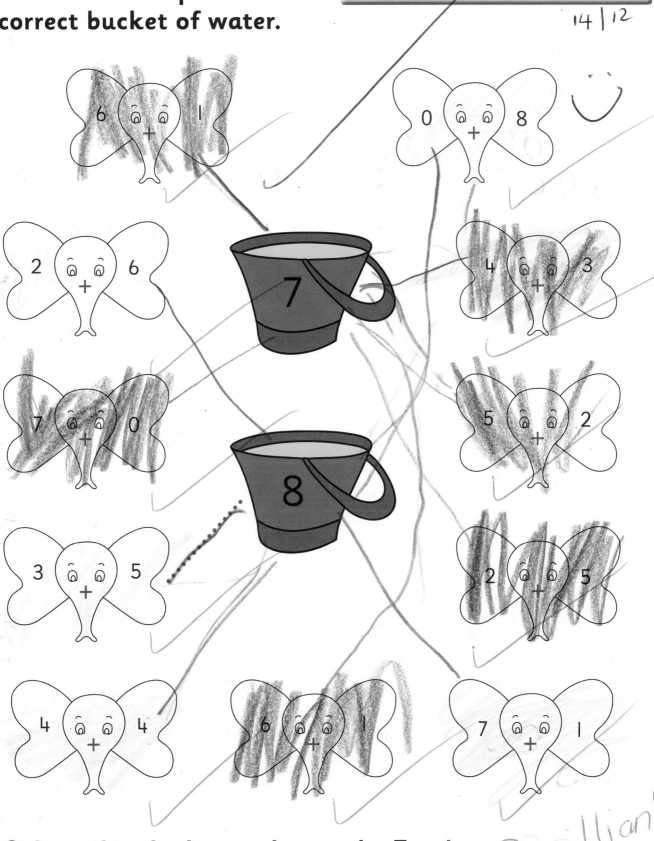

2. **Colour the elephants that make 7 red.**
   Colour the elephants that make 8 green.

Brilliant

11. Ordinal Numbers

Colour and Write

1. **Colour first** ▮ **, second** ▮ **, third** ▮ **and last** ▮ **.**

| first | second | third | last |

The 🐍 snake is <u>second</u> .

The 🐕 dog is <u>Lost</u> .

The 🐖 pig is <u>first</u> .

The 🐘 elephant is <u>third</u> .

2. **The first block is red.**

   Colour the second block blue.

   Colour the third block green.

   Colour the last block yellow.

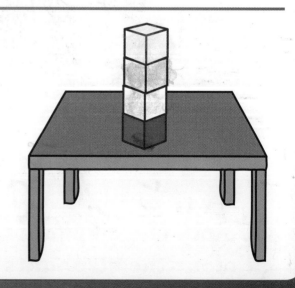

Strand: Number
Curriculum objectives:
Use the language of ordinal number: first, second, third, last.

Colour and Write

first	second	third	last

1. Colour first ▦ , second ▦ , third ▦ and last ▦ .

2. Ben is _first_ .

   Sam is _third_ .

   Mel is _second_ .

   Pat is _last_ .

12. Number 9

9 nine

1. Write the numeral 9.

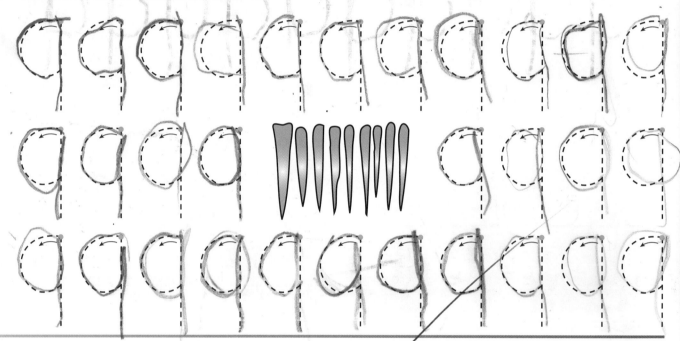

2. Colour 9 snowmen.

Strand: Number
Curriculum objectives:
count the number of objects in a set, 0–10;
explore the components of number, 1–10;
combine sets of objects, totals to 10;
read, write and order numerals, 0–10;
identify the empty set and the numeral zero;
estimate the number of objects in a set, 2–10;
solve simple oral and pictorial problems, 0–10;
develop an understanding of the conservation of number, 0–10;
partition sets of objects, 0–10;
use the symbols + and = to construct word sentences involving addition.

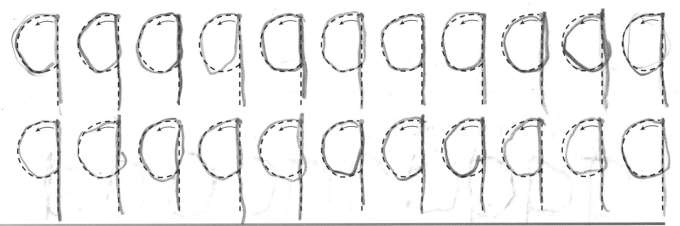

1. Write the numeral 9.

q q q q q q q q q q q
q q q q q q q q q q q

2. Ring the sets of 9.

3. Draw 9 snowballs.

Count and Match

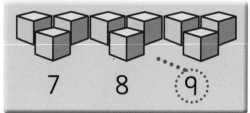

7   8   9

I.

7   8   9

7   8   9

7   8   9

7   8   9

7   8   9

7   8   9

Draw

1. Draw the correct number of bells on each tree.

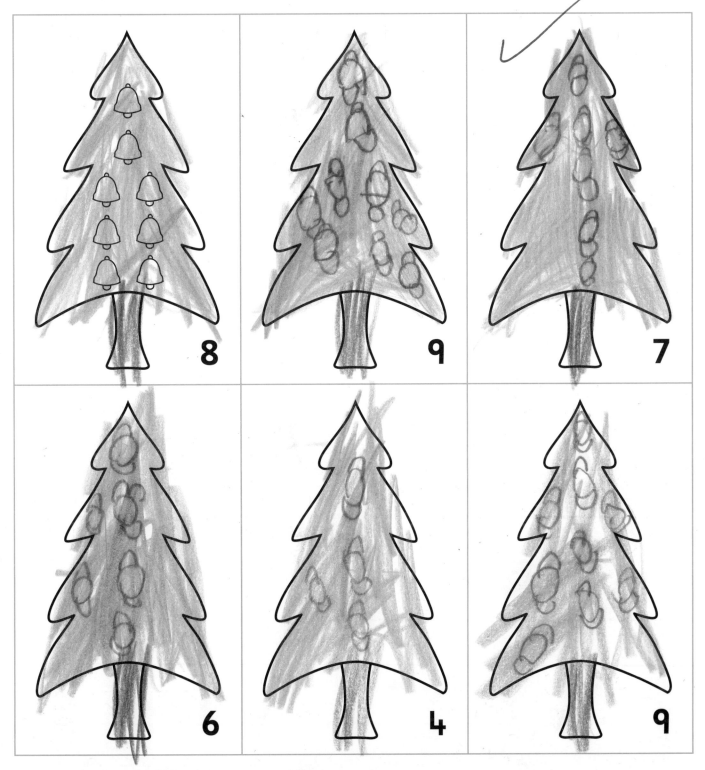

2. Colour the trees that have 9 bells.

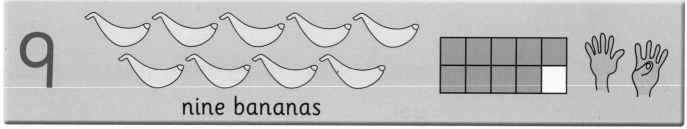

9 nine bananas

**1. Eddy Elephant likes to eat 9 bananas for breakfast.
Draw the bananas needed to make 9.**

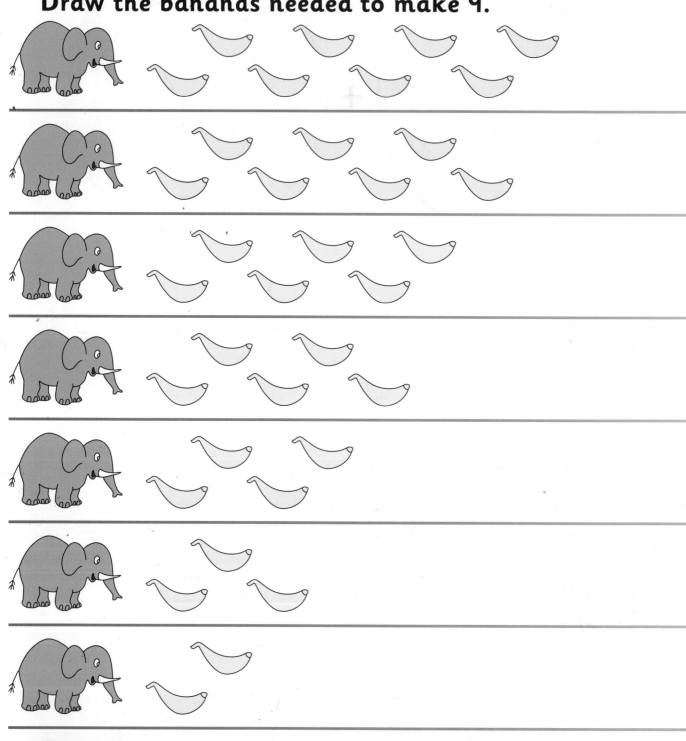

What Makes 9?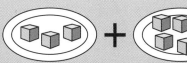

How many ways can you make 9?

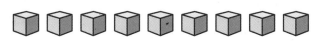

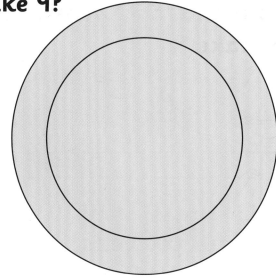 +

1.
5 + 4 = 9	4 + 5 = 9
0 + 9 = 9	9 + 0 = 9
1 + 8 = 9	8 + 1 = 9
8 + 2 = 9	7 + 2 = 9
3 + 6 = 9	6 + 3 = 9

2. **Colour 9 with two of your favourite colours.**

Make 9

Put 9 counters on the bell in different ways.

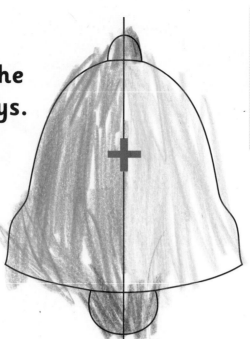

Use counters to help you.

1.

$$0 + 9 = 9$$
$$1 + 8 = 9$$
$$2 + 7 = 9$$
$$3 + 6 = 9$$
$$4 + 5 = 9$$
$$5 + 4 = 9$$
$$6 + 3 = 9$$
$$7 + 2 = 9$$
$$8 + 1 = 9$$
$$9 + 0 = 9$$

2. **Colour the bells that make 9.**

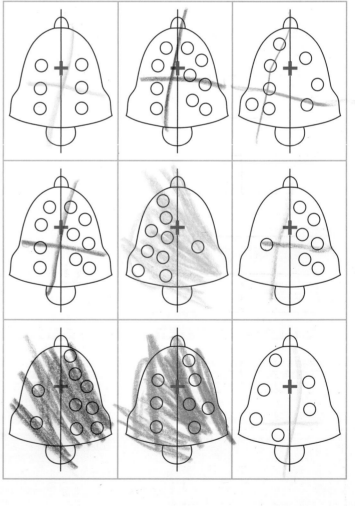

Add

1. Draw the counters.

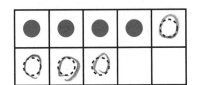   4   +   4   =

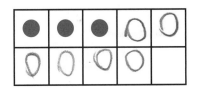   3   +   6   =

   2   +   7   =   9

5   +   3   =

8   +   1   =

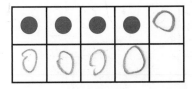   4   +   5   =

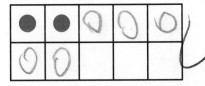   2   +   5   =   7

Super

5   +   4   =   9

Add

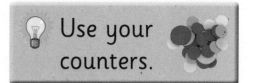
1. **Colour the owls that make 9.**

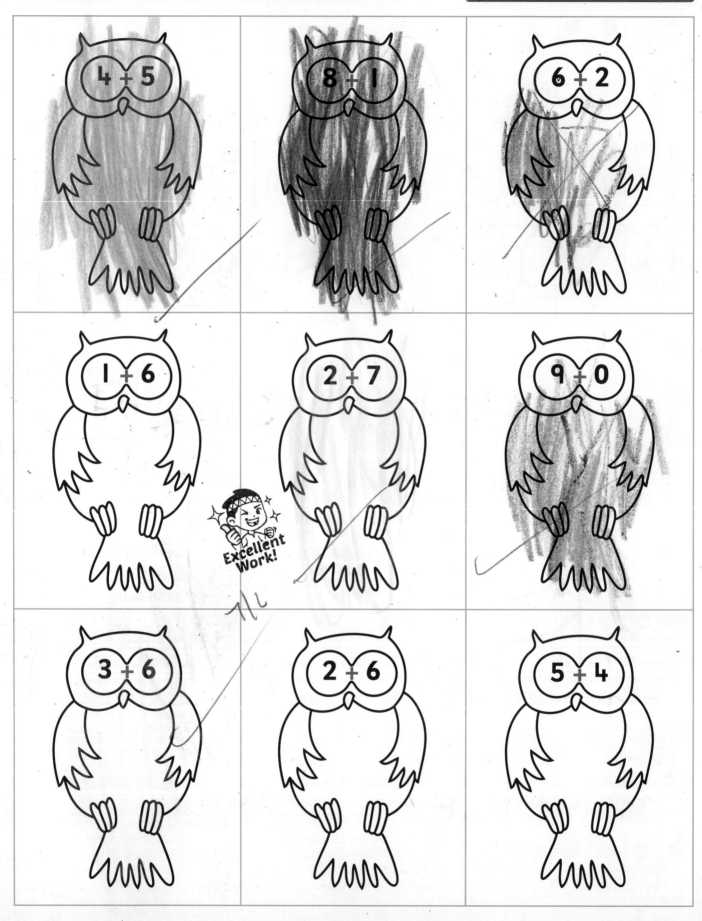

4 + 5	8 + 1	6 + 2
1 + 6	2 + 7	9 + 0
3 + 6	2 + 6	5 + 4

Excellent Work!

13. 3-D Shapes

Name the 3-D Shapes

sphere

cuboid

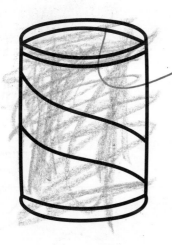

cylinder

cube

Strand: Shape and Space
Curriculum objectives:
Sort, describe and name 3-D shapes (cube, cuboid, sphere, cylinder);
combine 3-D shapes to make other shapes;
solve tasks and problems involving shape.

3-D Objects

1. **Match the objects to the correct shape.**

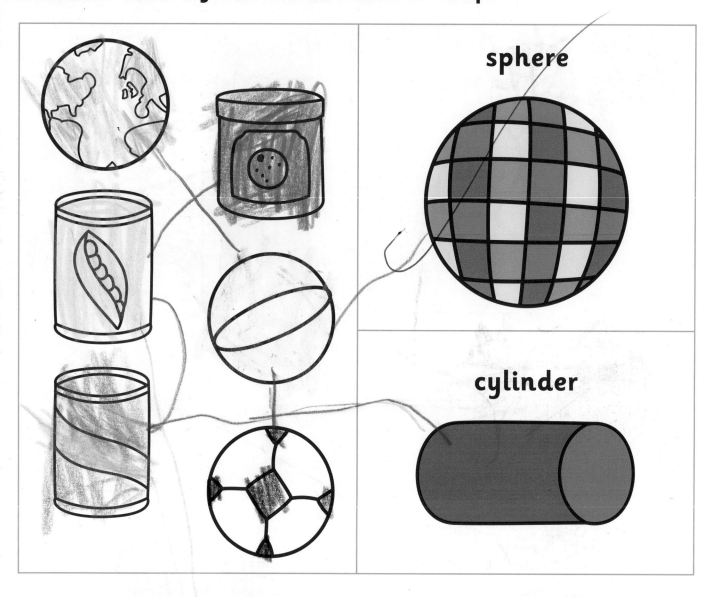

sphere

cylinder

2. **Find 3-D shapes at home and make a toy with them.**

3-D Objects

I. Match the objects to the correct shape.

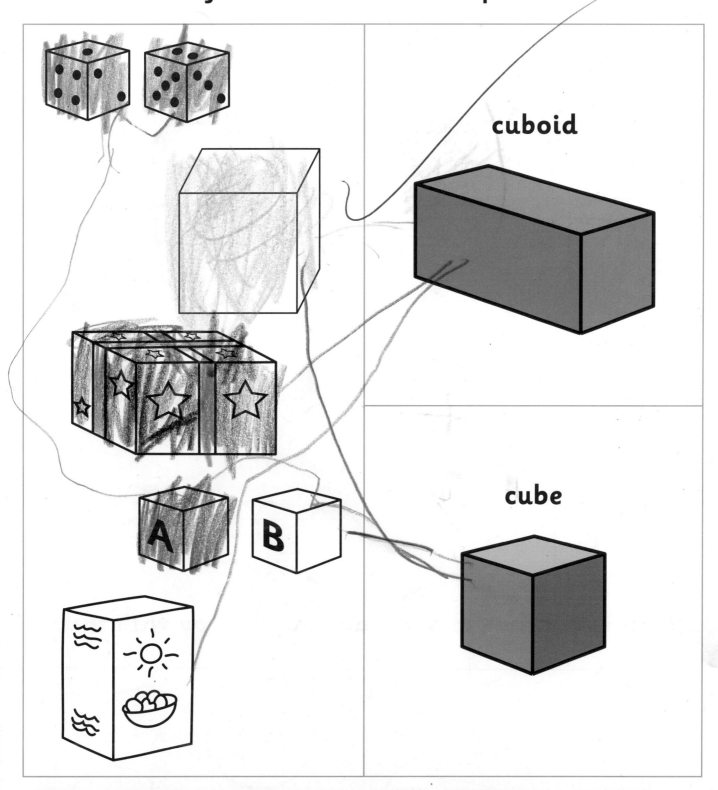

cuboid

cube

Challenge!
Can you make something with 6 cubes or cuboids?
Now try it with 8 blocks.

Sort

1. **Ring and colour the odd one out.**

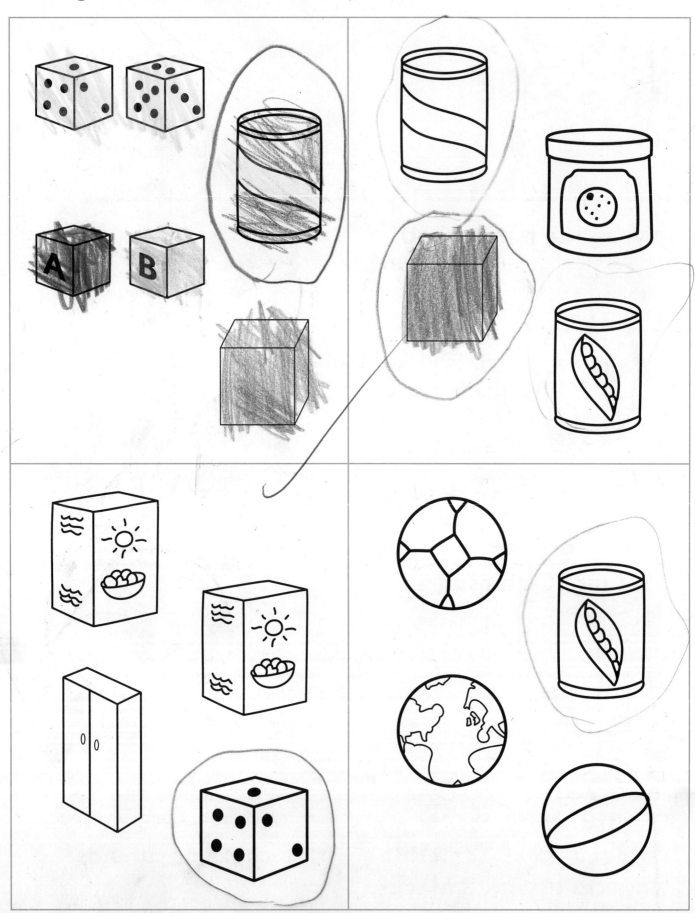

14. Number 10

10
ten

1. Write the numeral 10.

2. Colour 10 dinosaurs.

Strand: Number
Curriculum objectives:
Count the number of objects in a set, 0–10;
explore the components of number, 1–10;
combine sets of objects, totals to 10;
read, write and order numerals, 0–10;

identify the empty set and the numeral zero;
estimate the number of objects in a set, 2–10;
solve simple oral and pictorial problems, 0–10;
develop an understanding of the conservation of number, 0–10;
partition sets of objects, 0–10;
use the symbols + and = to construct word sentences involving addition.

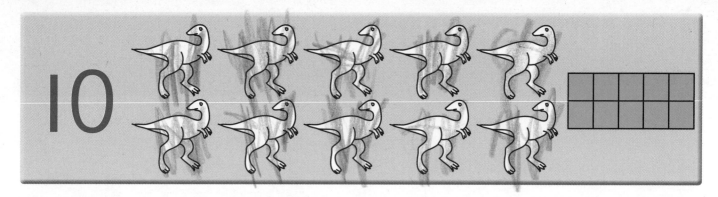

10

1. Write the numeral 10.

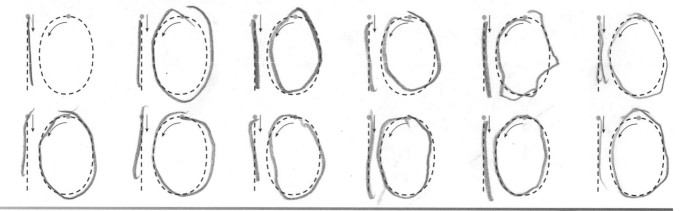

2. Ring the sets of 10.

3. Draw 10 dinosaur eggs.

Count and Match

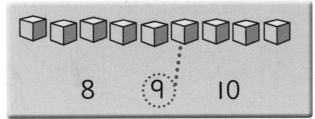

8 9 10

1.

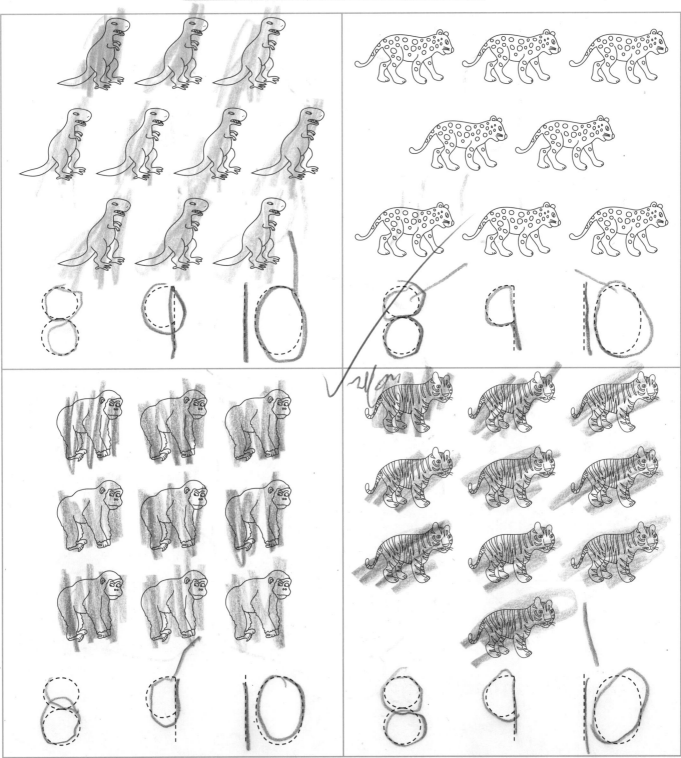

Finished Early?
Colour the groups of 10.

Colour

22/2·

1. Colour the correct number.

Draw

1. Draw the correct number of raindrops falling from the cloud.

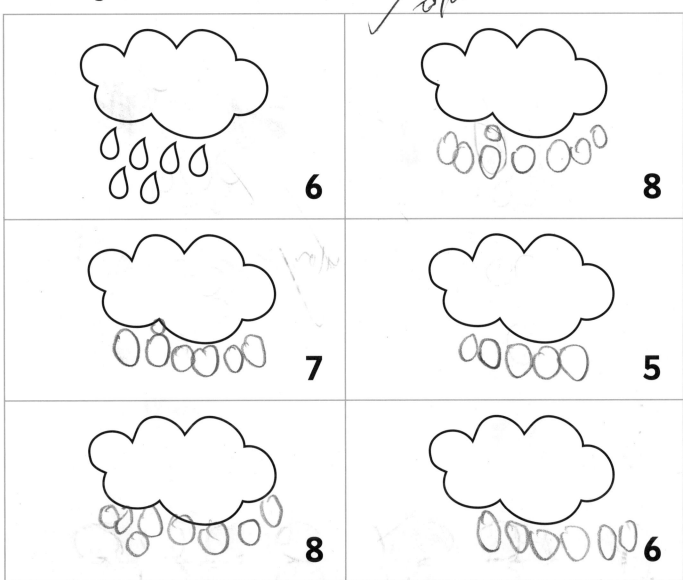

2.

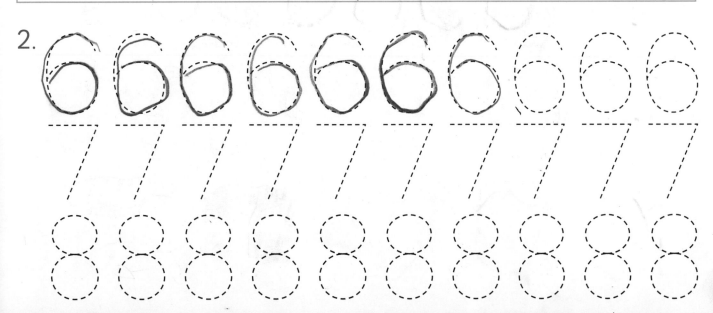

Draw and Write

1. **Draw the eggs in the nests.**

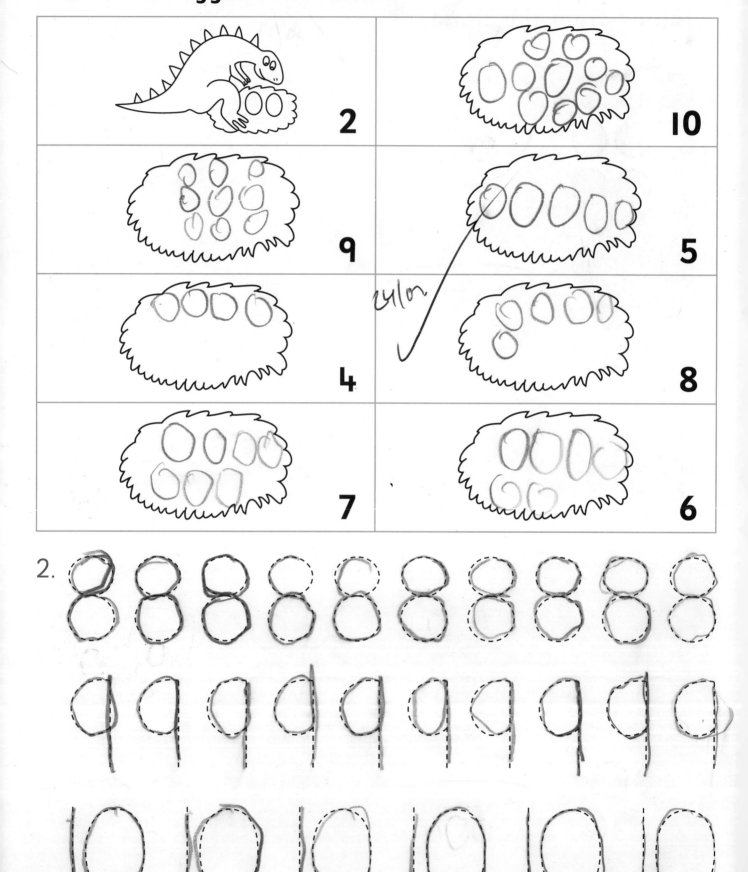

2	10
9	5
4	8
7	6

2. 8 8 8 8 8 8 8 8 8 8

q q q q q q q q q q

10 10 10 10 10 10 10 10

Make 10

1. How many are missing? Draw the missing counters in the bowl. ●●●●●●●●●●

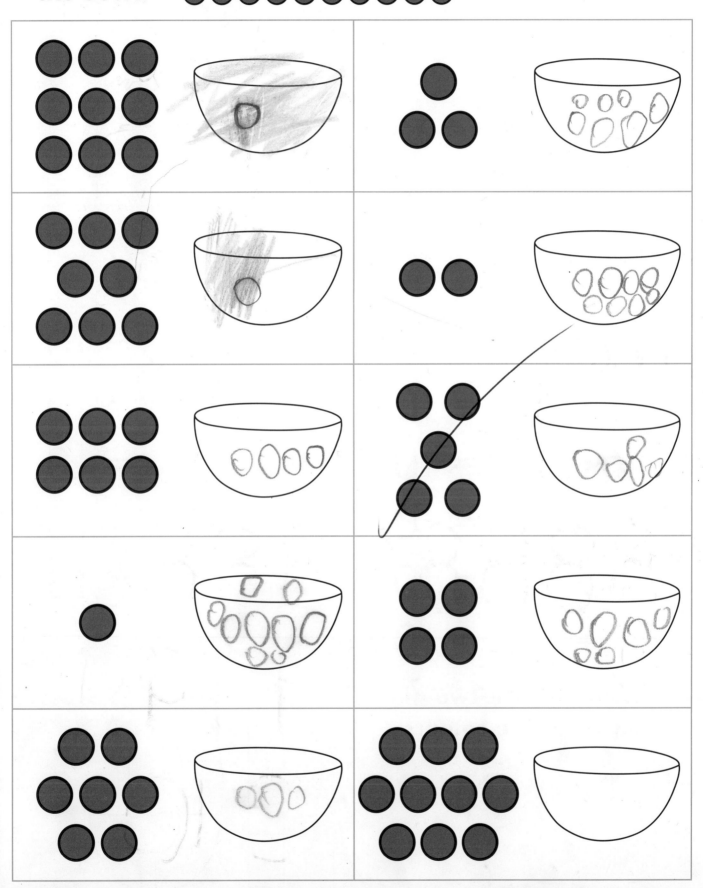

What Makes 10? 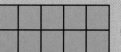 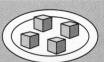 +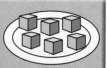

How many ways can you make 10?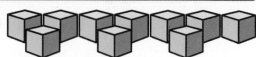

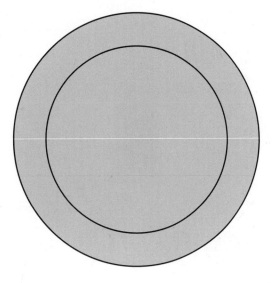 +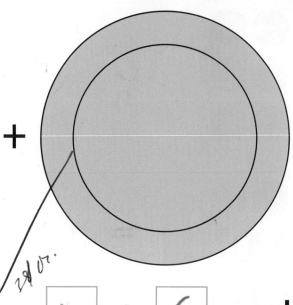

28/07.

1.

10	+	0	= 10
9	+	1	= 10
8	+	2	= 10
7	+	3	= 10
6	+	4	= 10
5	+	5	= 10

4	+	6	= 10
7	+	3	= 10
8	+	2	= 10
2	+	8	= 10
10	+	0	= 10

2. **Colour 10 with two of your favourite colours.**

Make 10

Put 10 counters on the elephant in different ways.

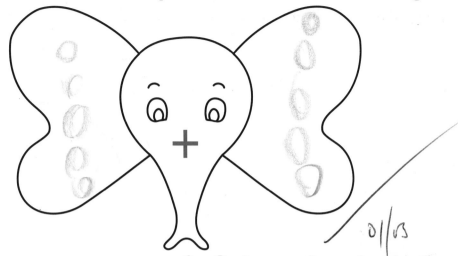

1.

0	+	10	= 10
1	+	9	= 10
2	+	8	= 10
3	+	7	= 10
4	+	6	= 10
5	+	5	= 10
6	+	4	= 10
7	+	3	= 10
8	+	3	= 10
9	+	1	= 10
10	+	0	= 10

2. **Colour the elephants that make 10.**

01/03

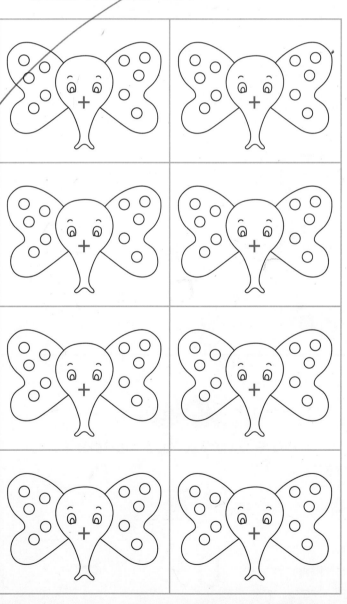

10

1. How many ways can you make 10?

$10 + \boxed{0} = \boxed{10}$

$9 + \boxed{1} = \boxed{10}$

$8 + \boxed{2} = \boxed{10}$

$7 + \boxed{3} = \boxed{10}$

$6 + \boxed{4} = \boxed{10}$

$5 + \boxed{5} = \boxed{10}$

$4 + \boxed{6} = \boxed{10}$

$3 + \boxed{7} = \boxed{10}$

$2 + \boxed{8} = \boxed{10}$

$1 + \boxed{9} = \boxed{10}$

$0 + \boxed{10} = \boxed{10}$

2. Add and colour.

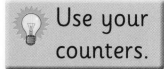 Use your counters.

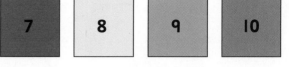

| 7 | 8 | 9 | 10 |

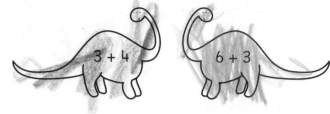

3 + 4   6 + 3

5 + 5   4 + 4

7 + 2   1 + 6

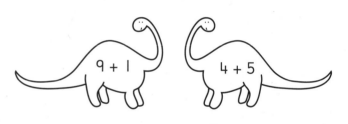

9 + 1   4 + 5

3. Draw 10 spikes on Danny Dinosaur.

Add

1. Draw the counters.

Use cubes or counters to help you.

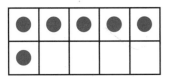 $5 + 5 =$ 10

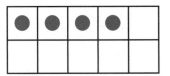 $6 + 4 =$ 10

 $3 + 5$ $=$ 8

 $4 + 5$ $=$ 9

 $8 + 2 =$ 10

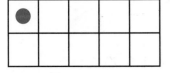 $10 + 0 =$ 10

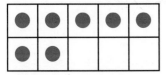 $1 + 9 =$ 10

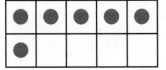 $7 + 3 =$ 10

 $6 + 2 =$ 8

$2 + 8 =$ 10

Add

1. Add the numbers on the jerseys.

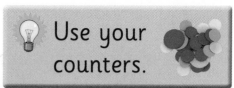 Use your counters.

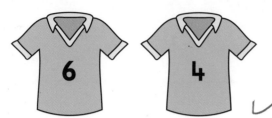

$6 + 4 = 10$

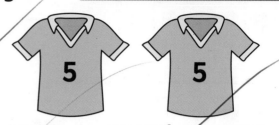

$5 + 5 = 10$

$3 + 5 = 8$

$9 + 1 = 10$

$6 + 3 = 9$

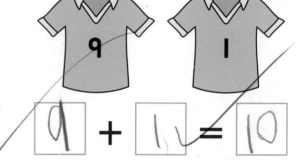

$8 + 2 = 10$

$7 + 3 = 10$

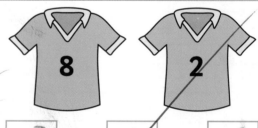

$4 + 5 = 9$

$2 + 6 = 8$

$4 + 6 = 10$

Add

1. How many more make 10? Draw circles to make 10.

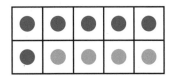   6   +   4   =   10

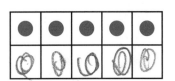   5   +   5   =   10

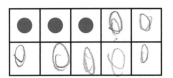   3   +   7   =

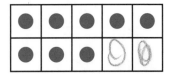   8   +   2   =

   1   +   9   =

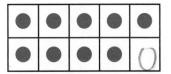   9   +   1   =

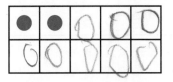   2   +   8   =

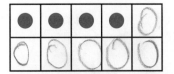   4   +   6   =

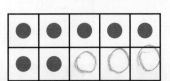   7   +   3   =

Colour

Colour the shortest.

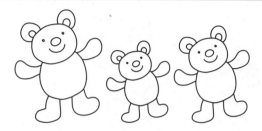

Colour the tallest.

Colour the widest.

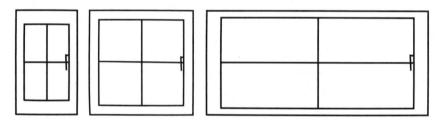

Colour the longest.

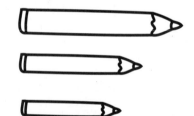

Colour the narrowest.

Colour the shortest sleeves.

Strand: Measures
Curriculum objectives:
Develop an understanding of the concept of length through exploration, discussion and use of appropriate vocabulary; compare and order objects according to length or height; estimate and measure length in non-standard units; select and use appropriate non-standard units to measure length, width or height and discuss reasons for choice.

Shorter and Taller

1. **Colour the shorter objects green.**
   Colour the taller objects orange.

As Long As, As Wide As

1. **Draw. Colour.**

Draw a snake **as long as** this snake.

Draw a pencil **as long as** this pencil.

Draw a window **as wide as** this window.

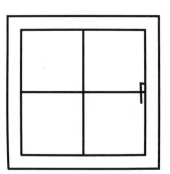

Draw a door **as wide as** this door.

How Wide?

1. Measure with cubes.

My estimate: ☐

My [bag] is about ☐ cubes wide.

My estimate: ☐

My [Cracking Maths book] is about ☐ cubes wide.

My estimate: ☐

My [book] is about ☐ cubes wide.

My estimate: ☐

My [tray] is about ☐ cubes wide.

My estimate: ☐

My [chair] is about ☐ cubes wide.

How Long?

1. **Estimate. Measure.**

	ring which one you will use	estimate	measure
maths book			
shoe			
pencil case			
school bag			
desk top			

More Than

1.
1   2   3   4   5   6

1   2   3

6 is **more than** **3**

7 is **more than** **5**

6 is **more than** **4**

5 is **more than** **2**

Great
2013.

Strand: Number
Curriculum objectives:
Compare equivalent and non-equivalent sets 0–10 by matching.

101

Compare

10 is **more than** 6

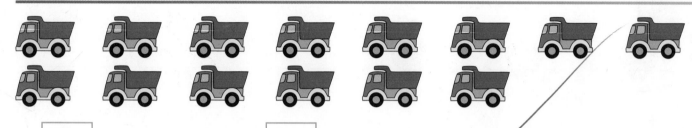

8 is **more than** 6

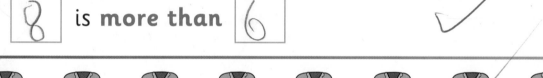

9 is **more than** 3

7 is **more than** 2

6 is **more than** 2

Compare

Mum has 6 flowers. Dad has 4 flowers.

Mum has ☐2 flowers **more than** Dad.

Pam has 7 bars. Jen has 3 bars.

Pam has ☐4 bars **more than** Jen.

Bob has 9 bags. Ken has 5 bags.

Bob has ☐4 bags **more than** Ken.

Jim has 8 bottles. Cara has 4 bottles.

Jim has ☐4 bottles **more than** Cara.

Compare

      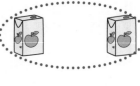

8 is **more than** 6 by ☐ 2

10 is **more than** 5 by ☐

6 is **more than** 1 by ☐

10 is **more than** 6 by ☐

9 is **more than** 7 by ☐

Compare

5 is **less than** 7

is **less than**

is **less than**

is **less than**

is **less than**

Compare

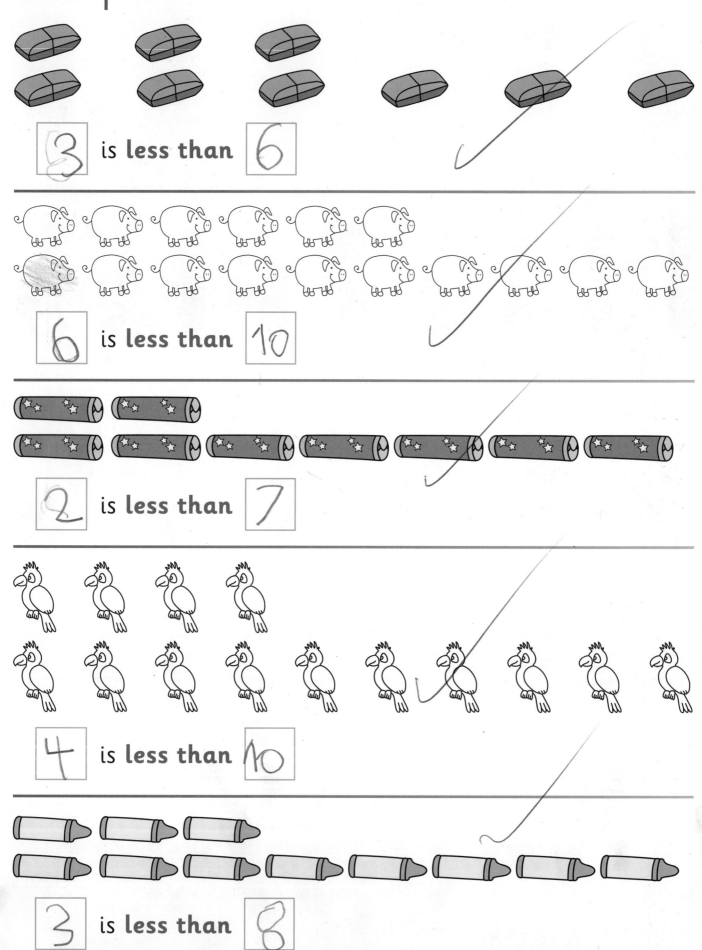

[3] is **less than** [6]

[6] is **less than** [10]

[2] is **less than** [7]

[4] is **less than** [10]

[3] is **less than** [8]

Less Than

Don has 4 buckets. Finn has 7 buckets.

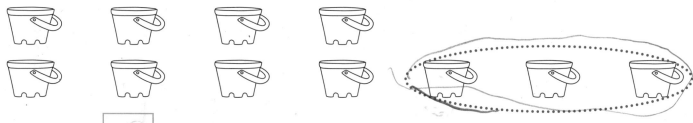

Don has [3] buckets **less than** Finn.

Jess has 3 baskets. Matt has 5 baskets.

Jess has [2] baskets **less than** Matt.

Jenny has 5 fish. Tommy has 6 fish.

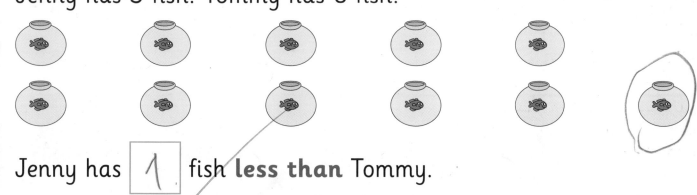

Jenny has [1] fish **less than** Tommy.

Kate has 6 jugs. Dora has 9 jugs.

Kate has [3] jugs **less than** Dora.

Compare

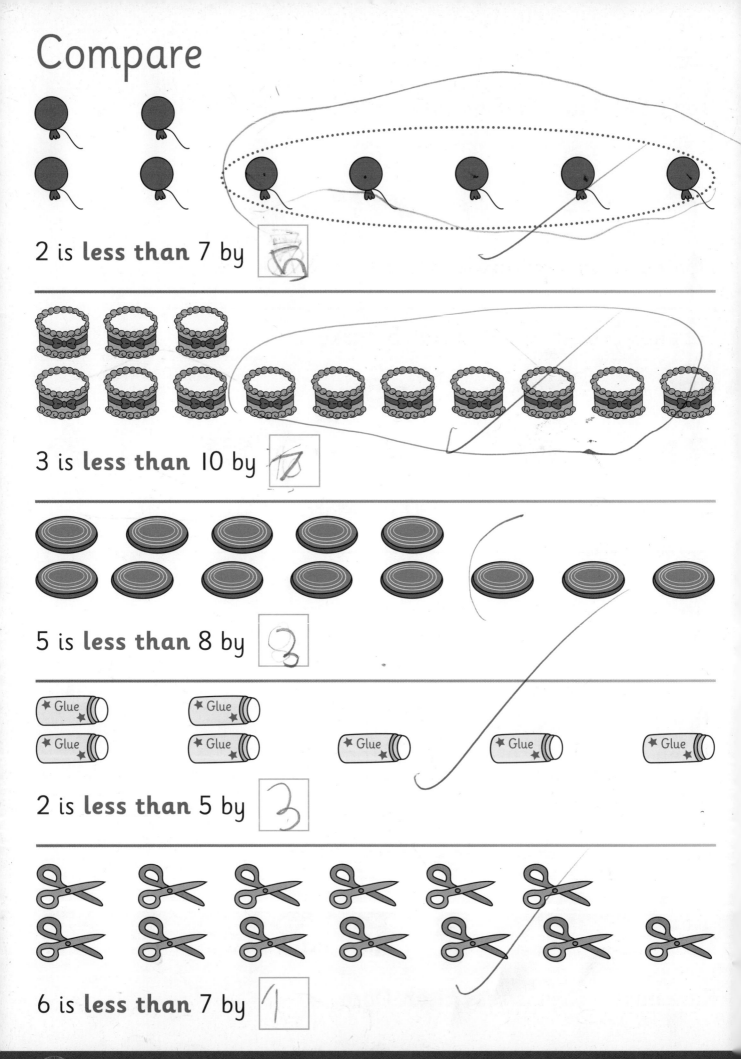

2 is **less than** 7 by [ ]

3 is **less than** 10 by [7]

5 is **less than** 8 by [3]

2 is **less than** 5 by [3]

6 is **less than** 7 by [1]

Colour

I. **Everything is mixed up in school.**
Colour everything from the art box blue.
Colour everything from the PE hall pink.

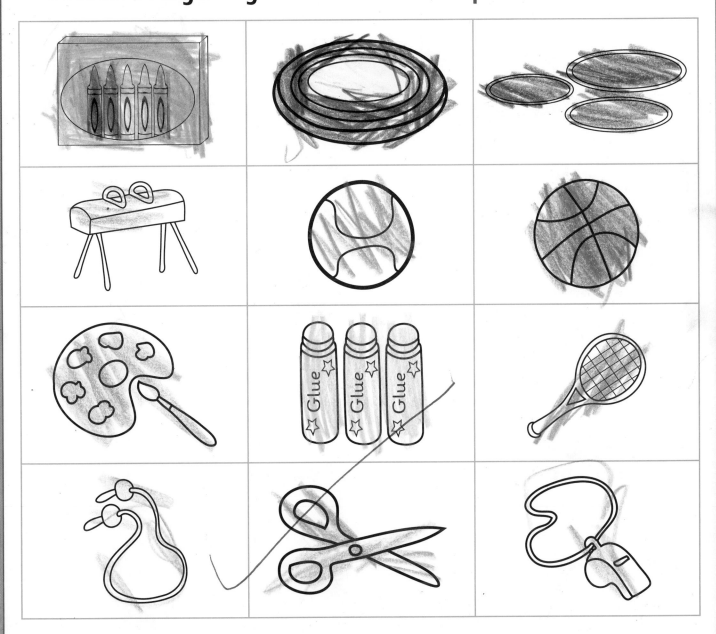

2. **How many pink?** **How many blue?**

Strand: Data
Curriculum objectives:
Sort and classify sets of objects by one and two criteria;
represent and interpret data in two rows or columns using real objects, models and pictures.

Balloon Fun

1. There are ⬚7⬚ **red balloons.**

   There are ⬚4⬚ **blue balloons.**

2. **Colour the correct number of boxes.**

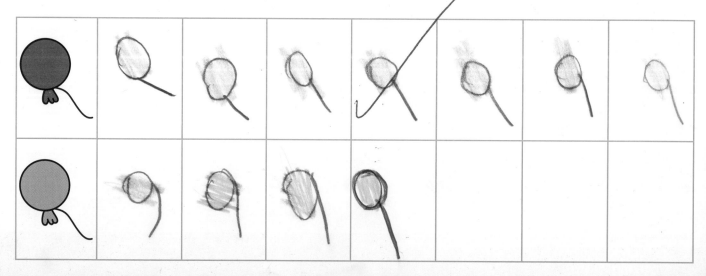

Pet Shop

1. **There are** 4 **kittens.**

   There are 3 **goldfish.**

   There are 5 **puppies.**

2. **Colour the correct number of boxes.**

Favourite Activity

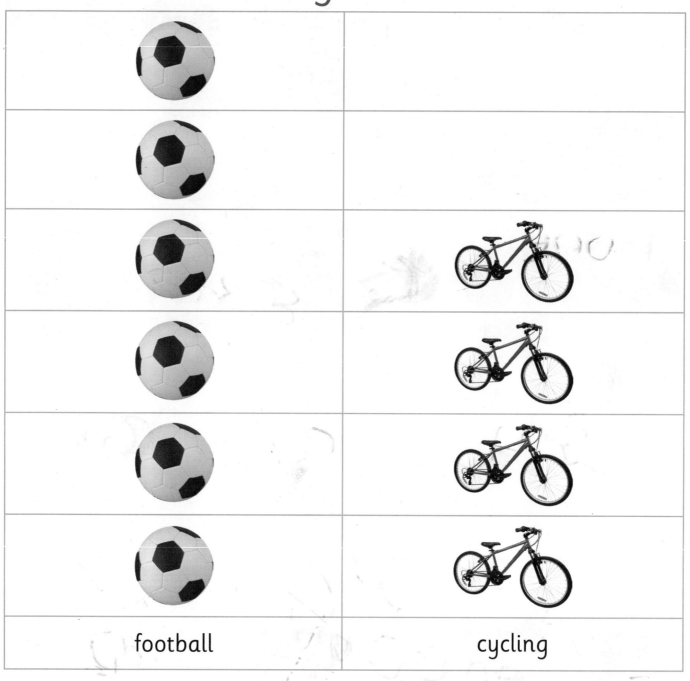

| football | cycling |

1. [6] like  football.

[4] like  cycling.

[2] more like football than cycling.

Write

1. **Write the word and draw the correct number of sweets.**

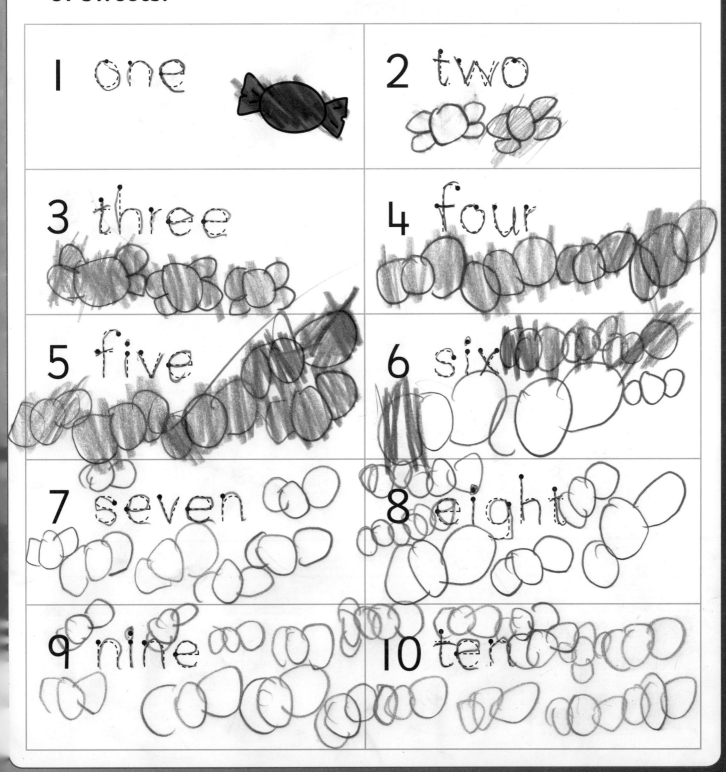

1 one	2 two
3 three	4 four
5 five	6 six
7 seven	8 eight
9 nine	10 ten

Strand: Number
Curriculum objectives:
Order sets of objects by number, 0–10.

113

Write

•	• •	• • •	• • • •	• • • • •
one	two	three	four	five
• • • • • •	• • • • • • •	• • • • • • •	• • • • • • • • •	• • • • • • • •
six	seven	eight	nine	ten

1. **Write the correct word under the jerseys.**
   Draw the correct number of dots.

_____   _____   _____

_____   _____   _____

_____ _____ _____ _____

Write

1	2	3	4	5	6	7	8	9	10
one	two	three	four	five	six	seven	eight	nine	ten

1. Match the word to the numeral.

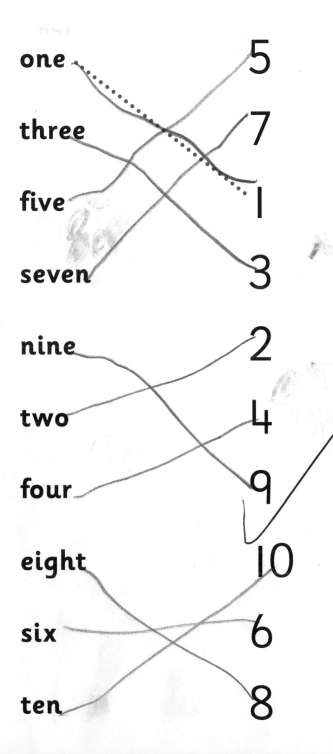

one   5

three   7

five   1

seven   3

nine   2

two   4

four   9

eight   10

six   6

ten   8

2. How many?

4   four

7   seven

9   nine

8   eight

Write

1. Write the missing numerals on the jerseys.

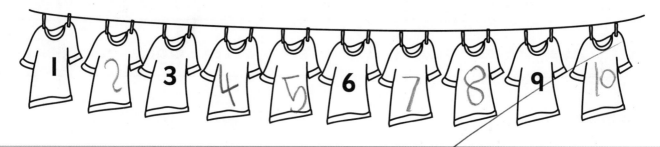

1 2 3 4 5 6 7 8 9 10

2. Write the missing numerals on the train.

1 2 3 4 5 6 7 8 9 10

3. Write the missing numerals on the caterpillar.

1 2 3 4 5 6 7 8 9 10

4. Write the missing numerals on the number strip.

1 2 3 4 5 6 7 8 9 10

5. What comes before and after these numerals?

V good
22/5

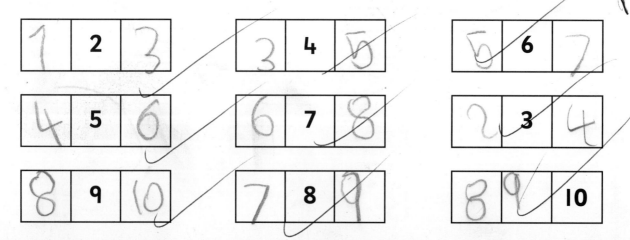

1	2	3

3	4	5

5	6	7

4	5	6

6	7	8

2	3	4

8	9	10

7	8	9

8	9	10

Comparing and Ordering 2

Light and Heavy

1. **Colour the light one blue.**
   Colour the heavy one red.

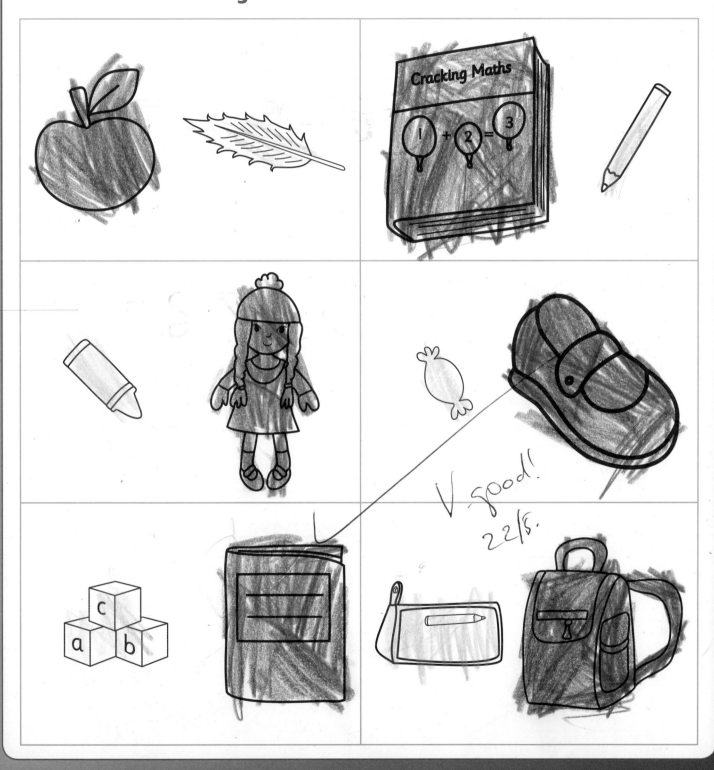

Strand: Measures
Curriculum objectives:
Develop an understanding of the concept of weight through exploration, handling of objects and use of appropriate vocabulary; compare and order objects according to weight; estimate and weigh in non-standard units; select and use appropriate non-standard units to weigh objects.

Heavier

1. Ring the heavier object.

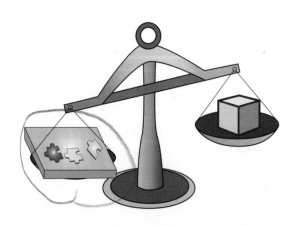

Lighter

I. Ring the lighter object.

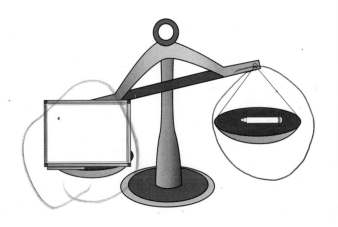

Heaviest and Lightest

1. Colour the heaviest.

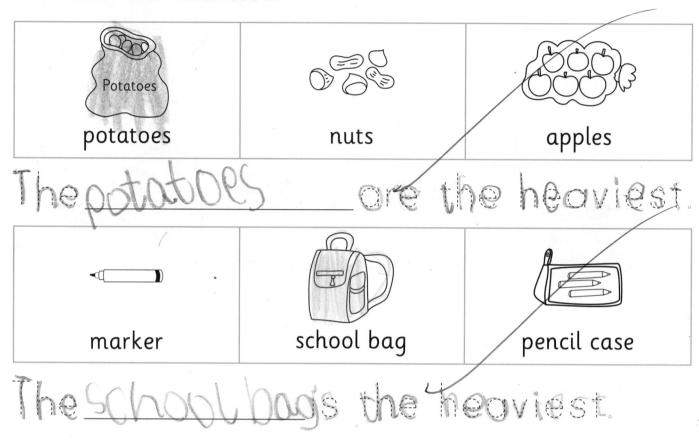

potatoes	nuts	apples

The potatoes _____ are the heaviest.

marker	school bag	pencil case

The school bag is the heaviest.

2. Colour the lightest.

chair	table	CD

The tabl CD. _____ is the lightest.

rabbit	mouse	cow

The cow mouse _____ is the lightest.

Weight

1. Balance with cubes.

Cracking Maths	My estimate: ☐ ☐ cubes balance my maths book.
	My estimate: ☐ ☐ cubes balance my lunch box.
	My estimate: ☐ ☐ cubes balance my crayons.
	My estimate: ☐ ☐ cubes balance my orange.

2.

Draw the **heaviest**.	Draw the **lightest**.

Add

1. Add on one more using the number strip.

6 + 1 = 7

4 + 1 = 5

9 + 1 = 10

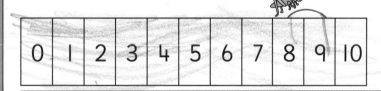

8 + 1 = 9

5 + 1 = 6

7 + 1 = 8

3 + 1 = 4

Strand: Number
Curriculum objectives:
Explore the components of number, 1–10;
combine sets of objects, totals to 10.

Add

I. Add on two more using the number strip.

$$7 + 2 = 9$$

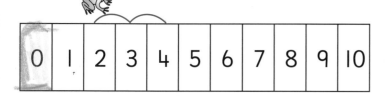

$$2 + 2 = 4$$

$$5 + 2 = 7$$

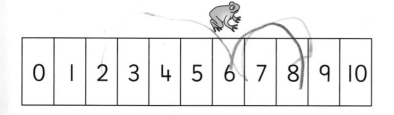

$$3 + 2 = 5$$

$$6 + 2 = 8$$

$$4 + 2 = 6$$

$$8 + 2 = 10$$

Add

1. Use your finger to hop on the number strip.

0	1	2	3	4	5	6	7	8	9	10

2 + 2 = 4   3 + 1 = 4

4 + 2 = 6   3 + 2 = 5

5 + 1 = 6   2 + 4 = 6

4 + 4 = 9   3 + 3 = 6

6 + 2 = 8   2 + 5 = 7

7 + 0 = 7   6 + 3 = 8

5 + 4 = 9   3 + 5 = 8

3 + 7 = 10   5 + 5 = 10

8 + 2 = 10   9 + 1 = 10

7 + 3 = 10   4 + 5 = 9

Analysis of Number

Add

1. How many robots?

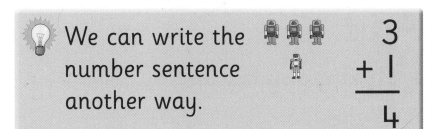

We can write the number sentence another way.

$$\begin{array}{r} 3 \\ +\ 1 \\ \hline 4 \end{array}$$

$$\begin{array}{r} 4 \\ +\ 2 \\ \hline \end{array}$$
6

$$\begin{array}{r} 5 \\ +\ 3 \\ \hline \end{array}$$
8

$$\begin{array}{r} 2 \\ +\ 3 \\ \hline \end{array}$$
5

$$\begin{array}{r} 3 \\ +\ 4 \\ \hline \end{array}$$
7

$$\begin{array}{r} 6 \\ +\ 1 \\ \hline \end{array}$$
7

$$\begin{array}{r} 2 \\ +\ 5 \\ \hline \end{array}$$
7

$$\begin{array}{r} 5 \\ +\ 5 \\ \hline \end{array}$$
10

$$\begin{array}{r} 6 \\ +\ 3 \\ \hline \end{array}$$
9

Add

I. How many fairies?

$$5 + 1 = 6$$

$$4 + 3 = 7$$

$$2 + 4 = 6$$

$$5 + 4 = 9$$

$$6 + 2 = 8$$

$$3 + 6 = 9$$

$$4 + 5 = 9$$

$$6 + 4 = 10$$

$$7 + 2 = 9$$

$$2 + 5 = 7$$

Add

 Use the number strip to help you.

1.

0	1	2	3	4	5	6	7	8	9	10

7 + 2 = 9	4 + 3 = 7
4 + 5 = 9	8 + 1 = 9
9 + 0 = 9	4 + 6 = 10
4 + 4 = 8	6 + 3 = 9
5 + 4 = 9	8 + 2 = 10

2.

0	1	2	3	4	5	6	7	8	9	10

2	3	4	5	6	7	8
+ 3	+ 1	+ 5	+ 2	+ 4	+ 1	+ 2
5	4	9	7	10	8	10

4	3	4	5	6	9	5
+ 3	+ 5	+ 2	+ 4	+ 2	+ 1	+ 3
7	8	6	9	8	10	8

Add

1. How many bones did Chewie eat?

| 3 | + | 2 | + | 5 | = | 10 |

   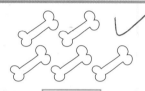

| 4 | + | 1 | + | 3 | = | 8 |

| 1 | + | 4 | + | 5 | = | 10 |

| 3 | + | 3 | + | 3 | = | 9 |

| 2 | + | 3 | + | 2 | = | 7 |

 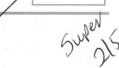

Super
2/5.

| 3 | + | 2 | + | 1 | = | 6 |

Add

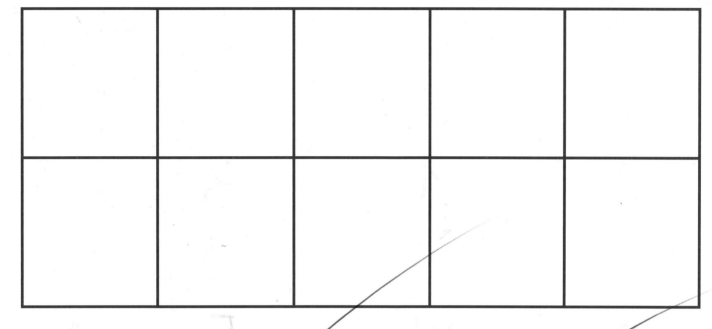

7 + 1 + 2 = 10   9 + 0 + 1 = 10

4 + 3 + 2 = 9   5 + 0 + 4 = 9

1 + 5 + 3 = 9   2 + 2 + 2 = 6

3 + 4 + 1 = 8   3 + 3 + 2 = 8

2 + 2 + 4 = 8   4 + 1 + 4 = 9

Add

I. Add the three numbers and colour the coat.

6   7   8   9   10

4/5

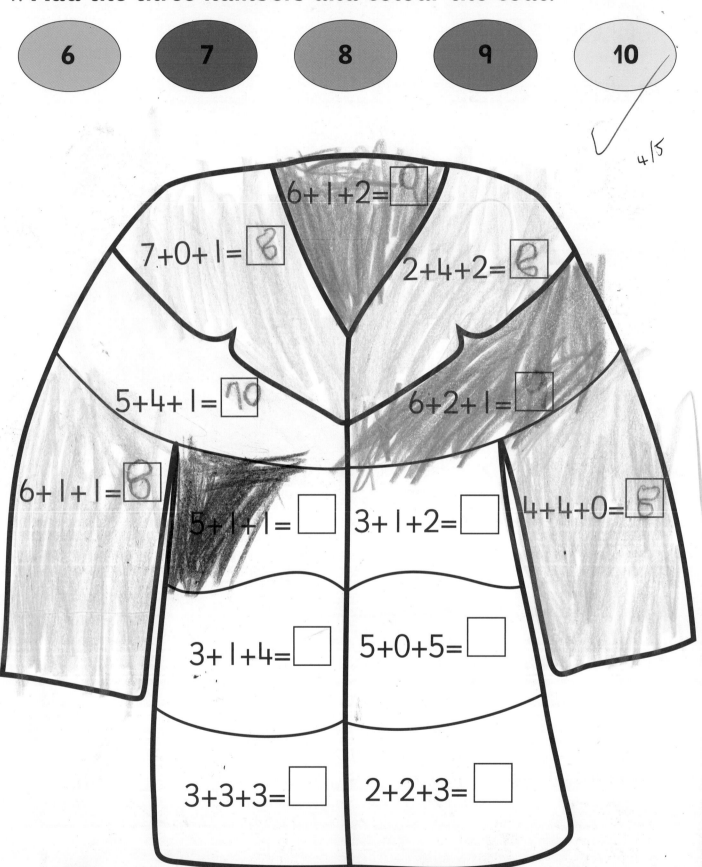

6+1+2= 9

7+0+1= 8

2+4+2= 8

5+4+1= 10

6+2+1= 9

6+1+1= 8

5+1+1=

3+1+2=

4+4+0= 8

3+1+4=

5+0+5=

3+3+3=

2+2+3=

Match

1. **Match the coins.**

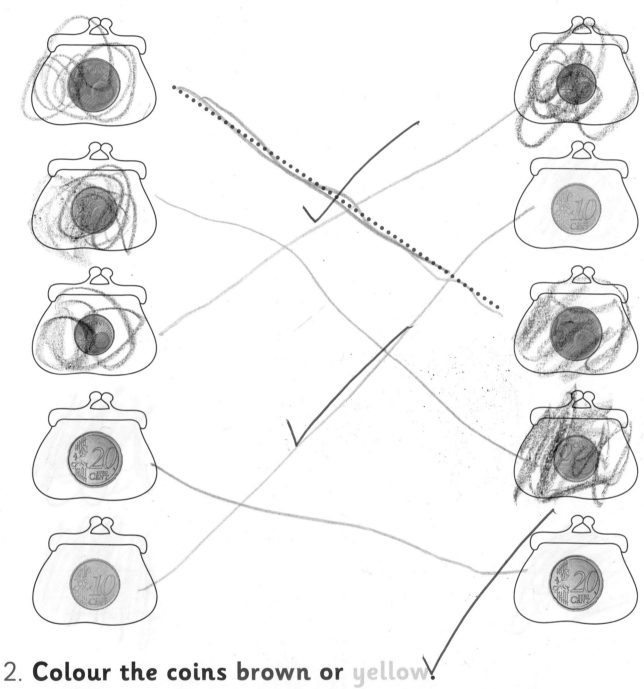

2. **Colour the coins brown or** yellow!

Strand: Measures
Curriculum objectives:
Recognise coins up to 20 cents and use coins up to 10 cents;
solve practical tasks and problems using money.

Colour and Draw

1. Colour the correct number of coins.

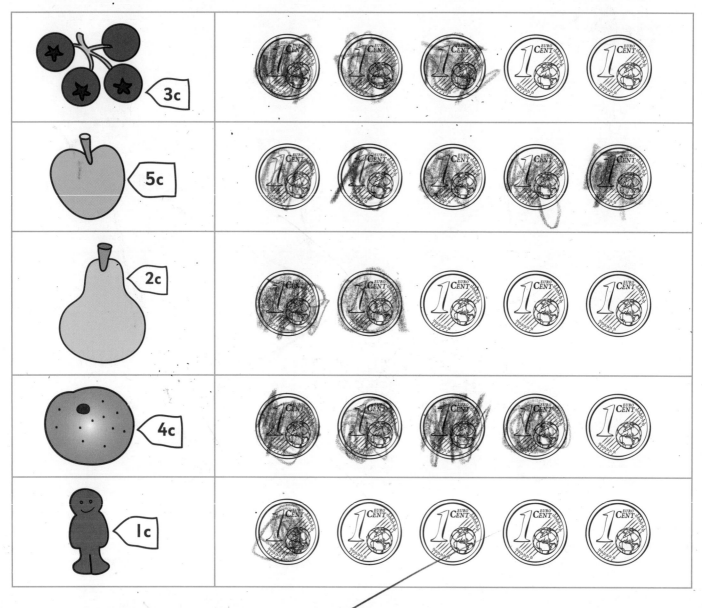

2. Draw the correct amount in each purse.

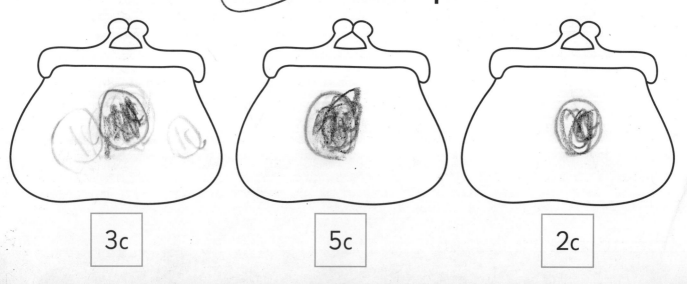

3c   5c   2c

How Much?

1.

John has 6 c.

Mary has 7 c.

Joe has 4 c.

Kate has 10 c.

2. Draw one thing that each child can buy.

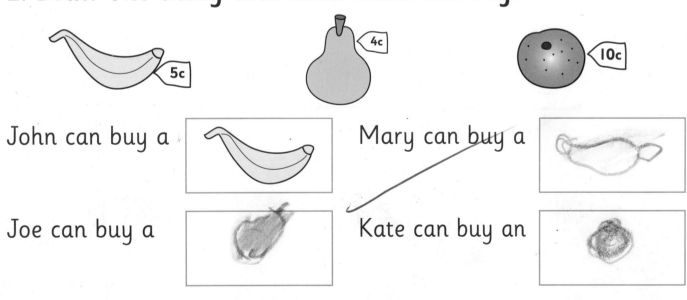

5c

4c

10c

John can buy a

Mary can buy a

Joe can buy a

Kate can buy an

Who has the most money? _____

Shopping

 2c  5c  1c  6c  7c  4c

1. Write yes or no.

 Ann has .	Can she buy and a ? ✓ How much do they cost? 5c
 John has .	Can he buy and a ? ✗ How much do they cost? 8 c
 Rose has .	Can she buy and a ? ✓ How much do they cost? 9 c
 Pete has .	Can he buy and a ? ✗ How much do they cost? 19 c

How Much?

I. **How much did Ann spend?**

$$5c + 2c = 7c$$

$$7c + 3c = 10c$$

$$4c + 3c = 7c$$

$$4c + 3c + 2c = 9c$$

$$6c + 2c + 2c = 10c$$

$$3c + 3c + 4c = 18c$$

Match

1. Match.

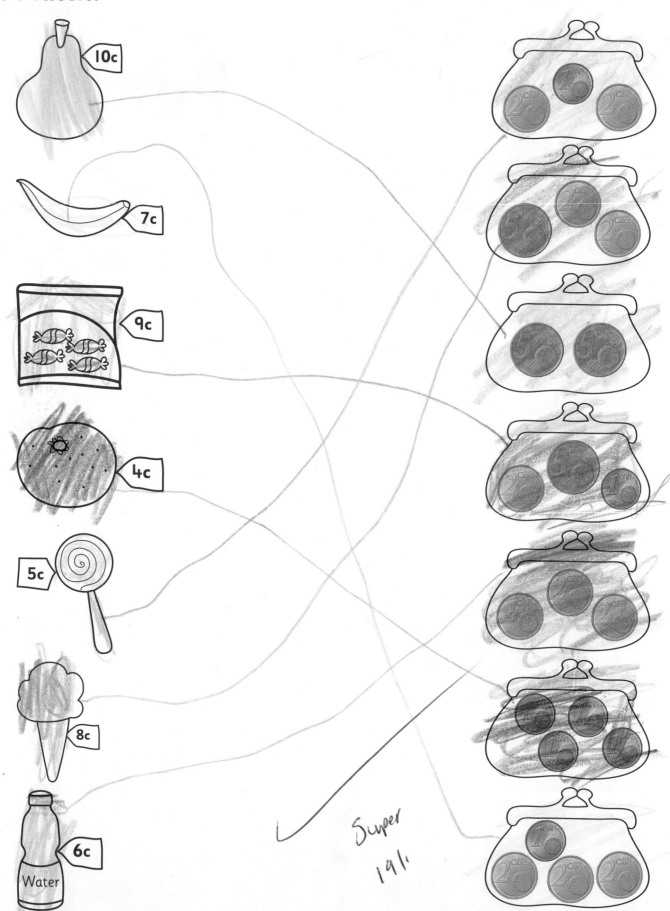

10c

7c

9c

4c

5c

8c

6c
Water

Super
19l

How Much?

1. Ring and colour the correct coins.

Shopping

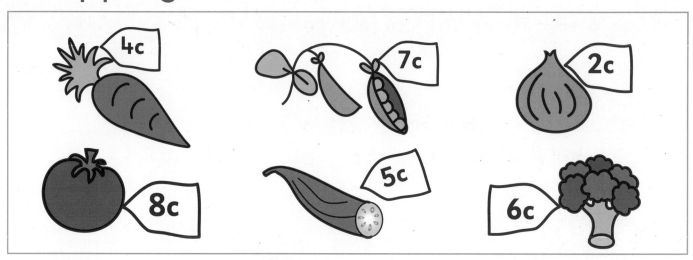

1. **What price is the** **?** | | c |

   What price is the **?** | | c |

   What price is the **?** | | c |

2. **How much change?**
   Draw the coins.

> Count on from the price to find the change from 10c.

cost	coins needed to make 10c	change
🍅 8c	1c 1c	2c
🥦 6c		
🥒 5c		

22. Capacity

Most and Least

I. **Colour the containers that hold the most green.**
   Colour the containers that hold the least blue.

Strand: Measures
Curriculum objectives:
Develop an understanding of the concept of capacity through
exploration and the use of appropriate vocabulary;

compare and order containers according to capacity;
estimate and measure capacity in non-standard units;
select and use appropriate non-standard units to
measure capacity.

Estimate and Measure

1. **How many** **mugs fill each container?**

	my estimate	how many mugs?
	4	5
	3	3
	1	1
	10	20

2. **Draw.**

The holds **more than** the

jug

The holds **less than** the

bowl